Praise for *To the New*

"For anyone who has ever been curious about life on [...] or fantasized about settling in."   —*Boston Globe*

"[Blais's] voice is intimate, loving, but the opposite of sentimental. She knows how to tell a story by letting the story tell itself."
—Joseph Ellis, author of *Founding Brothers* and *The Quartet*

"Blais writes with eye, mind, and heart in equal measure. I laughed aloud, teared up at least once a chapter, and sighed with recognition throughout. Coming to the end was as bittersweet as Labor Day."
—George Howe Colt, author of
The Big House: A Century in the Life of an American Summer Home

"What a pleasure—to be ferried to this storied island by an outsider-turned-insider, reporting so wittily and affectionately from the front lines of marriage, in-law-hood, real estate, celebrity neighbors and literary houseguests. How did *To the New Owners* manage to make me nostalgic for a place I hardly know? All credit to the heart, mind, and prize-winning pen of Madeleine Blais."
—Elinor Lipman, author of
On Turpentine Lane and *The Inn at Lake Devine*

"A highly readable valentine to a much loved [dwelling] . . . We find fascinating portraits of such eminences as the late Katherine Graham and the couples' good friend, the writer Phil Caputo."
—*Washington Times*

"Pulitzer Prize–winning journalist Blais affectionately recounts the summers she spent since the 1970s on Martha's Vineyard . . . Blais beautifully documents summers shared with family and friends enjoying unhurried days spent reading, visiting the quirky island towns, and basking in the natural environment . . . A bittersweet account of a wonderfully unplugged summer life."
—*Publishers Weekly*

"The Pulitzer Prize–winning author of *In These Girls, Hope Is a Muscle* (1994) pays tribute with affection and humor to [a] shabby but supremely well-located Martha's Vineyard house . . . Keeping nostalgia in witty check, while occasionally allowing it to shape a lyrical portrait of the place, she takes the reader on a verbal tour of the island . . . Blais fills her book with sentences to savor and memories so clear they seem to become the reader's own."

—*Booklist*

"A Pulitzer Prize–winning journalist and author gives a familial face to the mystique of Martha's Vineyard in this unfailingly charming reminiscence of summers spent on the island . . . An engaging tale . . . Much gentle humor and a certain elegiac sweetness . . . Touching."   —*Kirkus Reviews*

"Witty and charming . . . *To the New Owners* is full of beguiling stories and memories . . . A deeply felt memoir."

—*National Book Review*

"*To the New Owners* is a love letter to good times spent on Martha's Vineyard . . . Friends, some of them famous, put in cameo appearances and broaden the scope of this family memoir to something akin to a cultural history. Blais is a vivacious storyteller."

—*Omnivoracious*

To
the
New
Owners

To the New Owners

A MARTHA'S VINEYARD MEMOIR

Madeleine Blais

Grove Press
New York

Published simultaneously in Canada
Printed in the United States of America

First Grove Atlantic hardcover edition: July 2017
First Grove Atlantic paperback edition: June 2018

ISBN 978-0-8021-2787-7
eISBN 978-0-8021-8909-7

Library of Congress Cataloging-in-Publication data
is available for this title.

Grove Press
an imprint of Grove Atlantic
154 West 14th Street
New York, NY 10011

Distributed by Publishers Group West

groveatlantic.com

18 19 20 21   10 9 8 7 6 5 4 3 2 1

With love and gratitude to Nick and Lydia,
and in memory of Timothy Patrick Murphy (1982–2015)

Contents

To the New Owners

Chapter One
Blue Gold

We hoped the house would never sell.

Here is what I told myself: *Who would want this weather-beaten eyesore anyway?* I reveled in the house's inconvenient location on Thumb Point, at the end of a 2.2-mile-long poorly marked one-lane dirt road on Tisbury Great Pond on Martha's Vineyard. Maybe we could find a Realtor willing to show it only at night during a hard rain when the road was rutted, ideally in a vehicle whose suspension was shot.

Add to that a strategy of benign neglect: if you want a piece of property to go downhill, just leave it in the care of a bunch of word people. Decay was general: shingles had detached from the exterior like a self-peeling banana. Mice scampered inside the thin walls in the winter. In the summer, skunks slunk across the so-called lawn, a tick-infested wasteland of poison ivy and briars. The roof begged for repairs. The kitchen had mold. The faucet in the sink was temperamental. In fact, *all* the faucets were temperamental. There was no dishwasher. No heat. No AC. No Internet. No

1

cable. No TV. Many of the windows were either reluctant to open or refused to close. The sun poured in on hot days. The only relief came from the old black floor fan that listed to one side as if at any moment it too might collapse from heat exhaustion. The planks on the deck had splintered. Gouges lay in wait for innocent feet. With the exception of the master bedroom, the other bedrooms were small and, on hot nights, stuffy and airless. The house was in a flight pattern, making Friday evenings and Sunday evenings and Monday mornings more and more noisy, thanks to the rising popularity of private jets. In addition to those minor irritations, insert a major flaw: the fieldstone fireplace in the octagonal living area that blocked the view.

From our perspective, the more that was wrong, the more that was right.

At this rate, we were closing in on perfection.

I almost convinced myself that all the years my family had spent in this spot, all the memories, good and bad, were a firewall against anyone else ever occupying it. A dwelling that meant so much to us could clearly never have the same meaning to anyone else. By that standard, it was priceless.

My sense of ownership had a hypocritical element. The house did not belong to me, never did, and now clearly never would. It originally belonged to my husband John's parents and in recent times to John and his brother and two sisters. After my father-in-law, Nicholas deBelleville Katzenbach, died in 2012, we knew the property was on its own version of life support. In the months and years that followed, his widow, Lydia, had become frail, a far cry from her prime when she could command a room thanks to her contrarian opinions—with no desire to disguise them—and a bouffant hairdo that added extra inches to what was an already impressive-for-her-generation height of five feet ten inches. Now she rarely left her lodgings in an adult-care facility in New Jersey and she saw no reason to keep the house in the family, eager to see whatever sum it earned distributed among the children. In the end, the four siblings couldn't figure out a way to continue to own the property jointly. The three who wanted to sell all lived far away.

When I first met John, his brother, Christopher, fifteen months older, was at Yale studying law. I remember being impressed, thinking, *These people are going places.*

Chris is such a thoroughgoing lawyer that he once tried to mediate a dispute over a toy between two very young children. It was the old bad math that has threatened society since the beginning of time: two toddlers, one ball.

"It is never," he said, with perfect seriousness, "too early to learn respect for property rights."

Chris had gone to Stanford as an undergraduate, leaving for a semester due to an incident during an antiwar demonstration involving a rock and a window. He has always claimed that the charges of vandalism were trumped up: the fellow next to him at the demonstration was a varsity baseball player and the one with the good aim. During his time off Chris organized workers at Ford Motor Company, and much of his law practice has been spent defending employees against unfair practices. In the early days of AIDS, he specialized in getting insurance for workers who had been dismissed due to their illness. Chris has lived in San Francisco with his family (wife Kerry, also a lawyer, and children Cotty, Phoebe, and Hugh) for almost thirty-five years.

John's sister Maria (known as Mimi), three years his junior, was a member of the first class at Princeton to admit women. When I met her, she was in the midst of submitting her honors thesis for Princeton (supervised by novelist George Garrett) to William Morrow & Co. in New York City, which had agreed to publish it as a novel called *The Grab*. Mimi's book was well received, appreciated for the social nuances she captured when three middle-aged WASP sisters gather at their deceased mother's house in Georgetown in Washington to distribute her possessions in a family ritual from which Mimi's book got its title. The plot bore a strong resemblance to a process that Lydia had recently completed in the company of her two sisters, Elizabeth and Bunty, during which they drew lots and chose among their deceased parents' possessions—a ritual in which sentimentality sometimes beat out greed, and sometimes not. *The Grab* won widespread critical praise. Mimi wore sweeping robes of fabulous fabric. Although she did not ever appear to take so much as a sip, she sometimes had a glass of vermouth on her writing table as a prop. To me she was a Real Writer, while I covered Easter egg hunts and high school musicals as a young reporter. Years later, while on assignment to write about author Anne Tyler and Baltimore for the *Washington Post*, I had dinner at the home of book critic Jonathan Yardley, who asked if Mimi was still as striking as her jacket photo, taking mere seconds to locate the volume among thousands of books and to flip to her picture in which she was wearing a crisp white blouse with a hint of a plunging neckline. (She was.)

Anne, the youngest of the four, born in 1959, would soon be headed to Bard College, John's alma mater. She would grow into a woman who runs marathons and loves pugs. For a while, she supported herself and her trekking habit by working for

Patagonia in New York City, "catering," as she put it, "to the fleece needs of Upper West Siders." For many years our family's clothing reflected her place of employment. John was happiest when she was at Orvis and I was happiest during the Barbour interval. Her mind reels with wordplays, puns, and abbreviations. She never goes near the *New York Times* crossword puzzles, which get increasingly difficult as the week rolls on, until at least Wednesday. She used to attend the national crossword puzzle competition in Stamford, Connecticut. She said the secret is focus. One time the contestants were given a Shakespeare-themed puzzle and the woman next to Anne was thrilled: as a Shakespeare scholar at an Ivy League university, she had taught his plays over and over. Anne thought: *Cool, she will get so caught up in her memories of the complexities of each play that she will slow down and I will leave her in the dust.* (Anne did.) Anne's husband, Steve Knutson, worked in the music industry at Tommy Boy Records and Rough Trade and Audika. As a personal mission, he has devoted himself to preserving and promoting the work of cellist Arthur Russell, who died in 1992 at age forty. A *Washington Post* writer praised Russell for crafting both "orchestral music and left-field disco anthems." Steve created a foundation in Russell's name and attracted publicity in publications such as the *New Yorker* and *Billboard* and the *New York Times*. A museum may be next.

In recent years, both of John's sisters moved to Portland, Oregon: first Mimi, after raising her son, Avery, in Denver, and then Anne with Steve. Anne was the only sibling other than John who had been to Thumb Point after their father died. When the house went on the market, she stopped going.

John's brother and his sisters are voting, I often said to myself, *with their feet.*

They didn't fancy paying for the upkeep on a place they never used, looking at the profit from the sale as a welcome infusion into their bank accounts, helping to defray mortgages, pay school loans, plump up retirement funds, decrease credit card debt: the usual sunny side of economic life in America today. We were the only holdouts. We thought about buying everyone out and owning the house ourselves, but the math defied us. And even if we could have swung the buyouts, we would have to figure out a way to sustain ownership. Taxes and normal maintenance, without significant improvements, ran to about $35,000 a year. And significant improvements were looming as more and more necessary.

As it was, the months when the house could be used were limited. John's parents built it before the word "McMansion" even existed, at a time when people were still mindful of what the neighbors might think. They wanted a simple seasonal structure that blended in with the elements. They saw the house as a retreat. They opened it over a weekend in May, closed it over a weekend in October, and chose the second half of August through Labor Day as their personal time. They never envisioned the house as a replacement for, or as a rival of, their winter dwelling. Such restraint may seem quaint now, but it was once the custom. Roz Chast captured some of the pickled-in-time quality of our type of house in a full-page *New Yorker* cartoon in which she imagined a new attraction in Las Vegas, The Vineyardia, with "authentic-looking shingled roof," "seagull-and-wave surround sound," "complimentary pre-1980s paperbacks," "mildew smell throughout," "dozens of 'local characters' provided for your entertainment (nutty old heiress, crusty fisherman, bitter ex-famous writer, etc.)." For exercise, visitors could "walk on our 'beach' and look for 'shells.'"

My wishful thinking about the house's lack of appeal ignored the obvious. In truth, the house had charm. In even deeper truth, the house was on a peninsula, with pond water on three sides, leading to the ocean to the south. In real estate speak: blue gold and lots of it.

A house on a ledge to the east of ours was on the market at the same time. An old fishing shack with an outhouse, it billed itself as a "shackteau"—a term too cute by half. Built for duck hunting in the 1920s, the house was priced at $2,495,000. The ad in the *Martha's Vineyard Real Estate Guide* emphasized its authenticity: "No window treatments or painting techniques, no walk-in closets or kitchen islands. There are hooks for hanging things, enough counter space to fix a meal or two, kerosene lamps for just when you need them." Houses like it were rapidly disappearing on the island and I admired its endearing tenacity, like someone waving a flag for a country that no longer exists.

We managed to get two extra summers out of our house, three if you count the final one spent in dust and disarray dismantling its contents and lamenting the loss.

The moving company gave us some red stickers to place on the boxes and the furniture headed to storage. The intrinsic value of what we were taking was nearly nil: chipped Stangl Pottery, a rusty lantern that had collected decades of dust on the mantelpiece, two duck-shaped wicker bread baskets, a faded photo of Oak Bluffs from the turn of the twentieth century, a beach towel with a Ninja Turtle theme. The value of what we could not take was astronomical. How do you pack a view? Can you fold it up, smoothing out the wrinkles, and then protect it with Styrofoam peanuts? Was there a way, I wondered, to un-scatter the ashes of the people and the pets whose spirits we had set loose to roam the property, guarding us or haunting us, depending on their mood. A special sticker you can put on the fleeting nature of childhood or on the inner life of an oyster, mired in muck for much of its thirty-year lifespan, or on the smug superiority of a seagull with a crab in its beak? On how the ocean changes every day, as do we, but we only notice it in the ocean?

Better watch out, a friend warned when I embarked on this account, *you don't want to write the "Lament of the One Percent"*—a notion that made me smile. John and I met at the *Trenton Times* shortly after Watergate, when to be a reporter, whether at a small-town paper or something more big-time, felt like the most glorious calling imaginable. I have spent my working life at newspapers, mostly covering the disenfranchised, and at a public university, teaching young journalists how to do the same. Anyone who knows me knows I did not grow up thinking that a house on a quiet outpost with water galore on Tisbury Great Pond on Martha's Vineyard was my birthright any more than I expected bedsheets with a thousand thread count or caviar by the barrel. Far from it.

I do not fancy myself a crybaby. I had a strict Catholic upbringing with its firm conviction of the transience of life on earth. One of my all-time favorite overheard quotes came from a barroom philosopher sitting on a stool in the Green Parrot on Whitehead Street in Key West, who happened to echo my theology to a T: "Deep down," he said, taking a swig, "we are all on death row. Only the amenities vary." (Think about it: very few people would pick that as a *favorite* quote.) My father died when I was five, leaving my mother with five children, age eight and under, and another on the way. My childhood moved mostly in the direction of subtraction: fewer resources, lowered prospects. The nuns drilled us in the need for gratitude, for accepting our fate, for welcoming setbacks as a way to suffer on this earth to alleviate the suffering of Christ in retrospect.

So why was I, though not an actual owner, upset at losing what had never been mine? And where was my perspective? We live in a fallen creation. The summer of 2014 was filled with more suffering than we can understand: the riots in Ferguson, Missouri, after the fatal shooting of a black man named Michael Brown by a white police officer; the failed American rescue mission in Syria to find and free imprisoned journalist James Foley; the Ebola virus outbreak that began in the spring in Guinea, rapidly spreading into other countries in West Africa, including Liberia and Sierra Leone; Malaysia Airlines Flight 17 possibly shot down by Ukrainian separatists; thousands of immigrant children from Mexico and Central America warehoused in the United States; schoolgirls in Africa kidnapped by Boko Haram and allegedly flogged for failure to recite the Koran; bloodshed in Gaza; the suicide of actor Robin Williams. Every day a fresh harvest of sadness and discord. Did my time spent on this beloved property, this Eden—two weeks almost every summer since the mid-1970s—warp me? Did it lull me into thinking life could be different, easier? Did it take me off my game?

The sociologist Ray Oldenburg invented the theory that everyone has three places, the place where we live, the place where we work, and a third place where we are most truly ourselves, where we experience an unshackling of our normal reserve and sense of duty, a shedding of some no longer necessary protective hide. He identified the third place as semipublic in nature: a bar, a café in Paris, a bowling alley, a church choir. My definition is more elastic: a third place could be the bench in front of a piano, a fairway, a garden in full bloom, the bank of a river, a garage filled with tools, the reading room at your favorite library, a bike path near a swamp with beavers and turtles and blue herons. Our two weeks in the beginning of August was my third place, a dependable retreat, an annual tune-up, a lover's embrace. Pleasure was everywhere, from the smell of the taffy on Circuit Avenue in Oak Bluffs (who even thinks about taffy except on hot summer days?), to the weightlessness of swimming, to the drama of finding the perfect tomato and fingerling potatoes at the farmers' market in West Tisbury, to the mingling of limbs amid tangled bedsheets in the middle of the night.

On the island, I felt like a different, lighter person: more open, less burdened.

In fiction we readily accept that where a character comes from has the power to shape her prospects, for good and ill. Place often dictates destiny, but what about in real life?

Which comes first? The place, or the way the place makes you feel about yourself?

I was once told a story about a woman who had suffered a leg amputation as a child due to cancer. When she got older and traveled around the country, she elicited a different response depending on where she was.

In New York City, strangers spoke to her exactly the way you would expect New Yorkers to speak (high volume, no filter): "Hey, what happened to you?"

In Philadelphia, where she went to college, passersby averted their glances and never made intrusive or rude remarks.

In Miami, her hometown, as she strode down the boardwalk on South Beach, using crutches, moving at a remarkable pace, an audience of people, ranging from Jamaicans with dreadlocks and old Jewish ladies to Cuban refugees, University of Miami athletes, and homeless men selling palm frond sculptures, saluted her, gave her high fives and/or wide grins of approval, some even shouting: "You go, girl."

In each place she was in the thrall of an alchemy over which she had little control. Depending on where she was, the strangers considered her defensive, aloof, or gung ho, and she had not changed a bit. Or had she?

When we finally received an offer for the house we thought the family could live with, it was not as generous as our wildest dreams, but as a frequent guest, former *Fortune* executive editor Peter Petre put it, "Mr. Market has spoken."

The first encounter with the new owners was unplanned and fraught with misunderstanding. It was late June 2014, and we had come to the island to begin the process of shedding. My daughter, Justine, and her friend Madeleine were pulling out of our driveway when another vehicle, a big car with out of state plates, pulled into the dirt driveway in front of the house.

The driver stopped them. "Excuse me. Are you lost?"

"Lost? No, I live here," said my daughter.

"Uh . . . this is *my* property," said the woman.

"Uh . . . my grandparents own this house."

"I'm sorry, but we just bought this property."

My daughter and her friend were taken aback. They drove off, sending me a text to warn about possible visitors. Within seconds, I heard the sound of a car engine shutting off and doors opening.

A young (late thirties? early forties?) woman, trim and pretty, wearing a Hurricane Sandy benefit T-shirt, jumped out of the vehicle, followed at a slower pace by an older man and woman. One of two children stayed inside.

She explained she was the owner and these were her parents, having just arrived after a long day of travel by air.

It was late in the day, cooling down fast. The air danced with sunlight while the squawk of gulls provided an irksome accompaniment. Water rippled in the pond.

In turn, I introduced myself, likely using my husband's last name, Katzenbach. It is not legally my name, and over the years I have used it only if it created less confusion regarding our children or when I was on the island, where I found it cut to the chase. The family had fifty island years under its belt, after all.

After a quick handshake, I said that until the closing on August 29, not only was the house ours, but it could not legally become hers until we had cleared out all the stuff.

"Broom clean, remember?"

She said the real estate agent had given her permission to come onto the property whenever she wished. Was this possible?

"I wanted my parents to see the property."

Her parents and a child were standing by, polite and uncertain. Finally I said, "Of course, take a look." They fanned out onto the property, briefly crossing over the deck, scampering down some rickety steps to a path leading to the shoreline, returning quickly.

The land was indifferent as to who admired it, like a puppy who didn't care who played with it as long as someone did.

"We just got here," said her mom or her dad. "It's beautiful."

"Thank you for showing it to us. We'll go now," said the other.

The older woman reintroduced herself: "I'm Bertha," as old-fashioned and reassuring as a name can be. Her husband said they had come all the way from Seattle that very day. Solid citizens, not the least eager to be abrasive.

We also just got here ourselves, I wanted to say. *And those two young women along the road were my daughter, who just spent five years teaching in the Recovery District in New Orleans, and her friend, who just completed a nurse practitioner degree while living at home for three years so she could help her father care for her mother, who has had early onset Alzheimer's for years. They were not trespassers.*

I held my tongue.

Be a grown-up. No need to be defensive and no need for this encounter to end in antagonism.

I told the younger woman we would be on the island on and off all summer and she was welcome to visit again, but to please call first. "You might want to measure for curtains or something." I couldn't think of what else to say. It sounded normal, like borrowing a cup of sugar or asking someone if she thought a thunderstorm was on the way.

We did not know much about the prospective buyers, just that they were from out of state, the husband worked in finance, they had several children, and they had recently purchased the house of our former neighbors, the Es, as I will call them, two doors down. Their original asking price "during the height" (as people like to call those bursts of unmitigated prosperity) of $9 million translated to a little over $2 million when the transaction finally occurred. That house was also on the pond, with

13

a hot tub off to the side and a stone wall whose top had been decorated with rocks in the shape of hearts reaped, from what I understood, by Mrs. E during her walks. The rocks in the shape of hearts were all gone now.

The real estate agent had indicated that the buyers were unsure about what they would do with the property. Their children loved the beach. They might renovate, replacing all the old windows, perhaps removing the fireplace. They might keep the Es' house for themselves and operate our place as a kind of cabana/guesthouse.

It was all up in the air.

Before leaving, the woman thanked me again, apologizing for the disruption.

In light of this exchange, I struggled with whether it would be better to welcome the new owners or not. It was not unlike the classic question: Would you rather leave the island after a vacation on a beautiful day or on a crummy one? Finally I decided that in life it is never a good game plan to be a sore loser. This woman had every right to be as excited as she was for herself and her family, and when I saw her and members of her family spreading out across the property, I recognized that they would bring the same enthusiasm to it as I did.

As I pondered who might claim the cribbage sets that so pleased John's parents as a diversion after supper on a summer's night or the island-themed platter we commissioned from a young artist, I realized that what was perhaps most painful about the upcoming transaction was not losing the land. Land comes and goes; that is, after all, the history of civilization and its discontents. The hard truth is even if we could have afforded to keep the property, it was not the right place for us at this point in our lives. Our two children were grown up but not settled: forging careers, auditioning geography. It would be a long time before they had the freedom to spend substantial chunks of time with us on the island, and we wanted to be free to visit them and to travel to other places. And as much as we loved the house, we did not love its deficiencies, including a kitchen that made almost no sense (John's mom was no cook).

I often imagined a massive update or even a new structure. A second story would have been an affront to all our neighbors, and probably not permitted, but I always thought it would be fun to have access to the roof and turn it into an upper deck ideal for morning coffee, stargazing, maybe even sleeping outside in the fresh air.

My fondest memories are connected to the time spent watching the children grow up from year to year on the Point.

The first visit for our son, Nick, born in 1981, was at eleven months. Then we skipped a year: we could not see a huge amount of present happiness in spending two weeks chasing a two-year-old toddler who might dive off the deck into the poison ivy at any minute. When Nick had reached the sensible age of three, we were back again. Our daughter, Justine, visited in utero in September 1985: we were on the island for John's cousin Phelps Stokes Hawkins's wedding (three last names, very WASP). Justine was not so sensible at age three, and we spent two weeks begging her as she sobbed to put on her life jacket so we could take the motorboat to the beach. I still don't know whether what prompted the tears was discomfort at the bulkiness of the device or an aggrieved sense of fashion. Time plodded on, as it will, only to disappear in seconds during our annual two-week visit. Nick at five on the motorboat with his grandfather. Nick at eight, discovering the video arcade in Oak Bluffs. Suddenly he is eleven, with three guests, Ryan and Jason and David. A typical day for them would start at around eight: cereal, juice, cards. An hour later, they would re-eat, this time more elaborately, usually because an adult displayed breakfast ambitiousness while on vacation, cooking up bacon or a frittata or blueberry pancakes. Fortified, the boys would then take the motorboat out on the pond, or maybe the kayak, where they would pretend that a school of bloodthirsty minnows was after them, a phantom threat that produced real shrieks. Then they would have the first of two lunches, the one before they left for the beach, followed by the one they ate after they got there. They would be in the water in their wet suits with boogie boards virtually nonstop. Back at the house late in the day, they would occupy themselves before dinner with an obstacle course they had devised on the deck, accomplished by overturning every piece of furniture. They named their made-up game, which involved hitting a home run with a tennis racket wielded like a baseball bat, "porch tennis." They believed that their shoes, called Predators, gave them supernatural powers of locomotion. Later years brought more boys, Matt and Timmy and Ian and Dan and Ben and Marc and Adam. Same rambunctiousness, just deeper voices and, if anything, larger appetites. Porch tennis gave way to more daring deeds: the boys hoisted themselves and played on the roof, because they could. They jumped off the ferry just as it approached Vineyard Haven and swam ashore, because they could. Then the usual initiation rite of bad summer jobs with bosses who admire their own cleverness as they figure out how to withhold a paycheck from a novice worker. One summer the boys' notion of provisioning consisted of having at least twelve varietals of barbecue sauce on hand at all times.

Justine and her friends benefited from being around the boys, principally during throwing contests in the water to see how high they could be tossed. Three girls in particular were fixtures: two sisters, Claire and Hilary Lawlor (pronounced *Lahlah*), who had a house in Oak Bluffs, and Jen Tyson, a frequent houseguest of Claire and Hilary's family, including during adolescence when she would come to the island and work at the Stop & Shop in Edgartown.

My favorite example of the sibling dynamic comes from when Claire and Hilary were little and being driven around the countryside in their parents' minivan. Claire claimed that any horses they saw belonged to her, but Hilary could have all the cows. Claire also convinced Hilary that she had superpowers and if she ran fast enough she could run through walls, with nearly disastrous effect. Nick enacted his own older sibling power play when Justine was around seven, scrawny as can be, and he coaxed her into stepping up to the counter at Mad Martha's on her own to say the magic word "OINK" and order a magnificent concoction while the others hid. That way it looked as if she were going to eat twelve scoops of ice cream with unlimited sauces and toppings on her own.

Justine's summers meant fireworks at the Lewises', bridge-jumping in Oak Bluffs, serving as sous chef to our guest Phil Caputo when he decided it was time to re-create one of his grandmother's classic Italian recipes. At sixteen, a rash and sudden fatigue—perhaps a case of Lyme disease? After googling it, and learning that "personality changes" are among the possible side effects, a torrent of tears: for a teenaged girl, an unbearable prospect. She was saved by the right medication administered in a timely fashion. A summer during college for Claire and Justine at a surf shop, the Boneyard, working retail. Customer: "What's the difference between a large and an extra large?" Answer: "Um, one is larger than the other?"

What was most vexing to me about selling the house was that the new owners had no idea what they were getting. They saw 5.5 acres, with only a small portion a buildable footprint. They saw the lot and the subdivision numbers by which we were known to the town of West Tisbury, important if it ever had to send a fire engine our way. They saw a roof that needed replacing and the chance to burden us with half the cost ($17,000). They saw a house they might upgrade, a house they might tear down.

The new owners could of course imagine their own future happiness, but they could not see, and therefore could not appreciate, the human history preceding the purchase, all the lives that grazed ours and the ones that truly intersected, the noisy arrivals and departures, the arguments and the recipes, the ghosts and the guests, crabs caught and birthdays celebrated, clams shucked, towels shaken, lures assembled, bonfires lit, the dogs we indulged, the ticks we cursed, the pies we consumed, and, through it all, both close by and in the distance, the moving waters (as a poet put it) at their priestlike task. They could not see the depth of the life lived here during the summer for all those years.

Chapter Two

The Shack

John and I met in New Jersey during the 1970s, a skittish time in the history of the republic, the era that brought us leisure suits, *Charlie's Angels*, sideburns, Studio 54, wide ties and even wider lapels. We were both reporters at the *Trenton Times*, a sleepy afternoon newspaper in an even sleepier state capital known as a manufacturing hub in its heyday, famous for ceramics, oyster crackers, and condoms (a prominent sign on a bridge declared, TRENTON MAKES, THE WORLD TAKES). The paper had recently been purchased by the *Washington Post*, in what proved to be an ill-thought-out act of post-Watergate colonialism, for the express purpose of taking on the *New York Times* in its own "backyard." This was not going to be easy. We soon got to joking that the city motto should be "Dare to be complacent." Trenton was a Balkanized town with ethnic enclaves, resistant to change and to scrutiny.

I was afraid I had made a bad trade, moving from Massachusetts, home of the Cabots and the Lowells, boiled food, and chronic understatement, to New Jersey, the Bad Taste State.

In order to do my job, I needed to buy a car, and the editor asked if I wanted a foreign car or an American model. I wasn't sure. He pointed out a guy named Harry—short, middle-aged, with a crew cut; married with four children and a house in the suburbs—the American car expert in that he covered the Trenton Speedway. He pointed out a guy named John—single, young, lanky—the foreign car expert in that he had a foreign car that was always breaking down in the company parking lot.

Easy: "Foreign."

Thus the first indelible image of my future husband was the look of panic on his face in the rearview mirror as I careened down Perry Street in an orange VW Dasher with the word DASHER in huge black letters on the side, gears grinding, the equally terrified salesman riding shotgun.

If there was commonality between John and me, it was that we were both readers and we possessed the personality of readers, introverts with a secret desire to be swept away, especially within the safe confines of a many-hundred-paged book. John had a red leather chair that was losing its innards on a daily basis, hemorrhaging foam and coils, which he often sank into to read the stack of hardcover books at its feet. I was drawn to him for the generic reasons that made him the ideal choice to help me pick out a car (see: *single, young, lanky*), but eventually, specifically, because of that chair. I was deep in the thrall of the certitude that a man who reads is not all brute. He had me at the stack of books, but that wasn't all. Our first date was to see a remake of the movie *The Front Page*, and John's even better idea of a second date was to suggest we go hear this up-and-coming singer from Asbury Park, New Jersey, Bruce Somebody, who was performing at the civic center in Trenton.

After that our courtship took a literal turn, when we went as often as possible to some rarely used public tennis courts in West Amwell, where John undertook a daunting task. He tried to teach *me* how to hit a ball. After automotive need, he is most moved by the desire to correct athletic deficits. In an unwitting way, I must have seemed the beau ideal. He forgave me my ineptitude in tennis, and I forgave him his housekeeping skills, which featured empty grocery bags tossed all over the kitchen, and I also promised not to disparage the contents of his fridge, a single guy's dream smorgasbord of soda, beer, ham, cheese, white bread, iceberg lettuce, and Hellmann's mayonnaise in jumbo jars. John lived in Hopewell, New Jersey, scene of the Lindbergh kidnapping, across from a tiny commuter train station at 27 Railroad Place in a somewhat confused effort to move to either the right side or the wrong side of the tracks: I was never entirely certain.

The differences between John's family and mine are easy to document in broad reductive strokes: they are before the *Mayflower*, mine is before the potato famine; Princeton University and Bennington College, the College of the Holy Cross and Bridgewater State Teachers College; private viewings of the movie *PT 109* at the White House, all-you-can-eat spaghetti suppers in the church basement. One carefree summer, John toured Europe with his father and his older brother in a Triumph TR3 sports car. My family routinely piled into my mother's wheezing Nash Rambler station wagon and stuck to nearby errands: the purchase of homemade turkey pies, Child's in Holyoke for shoes twice a year (school and Easter), a farm stand to buy peonies in season. John's father was mythic because he was part of history; mine was mythic because he was dead.

The small farming community in Massachusetts where I grew up might as well have been in the Midwest in the way it exulted in the deep rhythms of its ordinariness. Horses, cows, corn, the Grange Fair, and a certain kind of old-style skinflint Republicanism were all familiar to me. As Irish Catholics and as Democrats, our widowed mother and her six children were "the other." In a place that valued tools and thrift, we had an air of eccentricity, trailed by the unspoken question: *How do they manage, after all?*

Viewed in the extreme, I feared my family and I might be construed as loud, freckled, ditty-whistling, parade-going, whiskey-swilling, cabbage-eating, catechism-memorizing, superstition-believing, fight-song-singing, body-and-blood-swallowing slaves of the Vatican. The opposite was a truer picture: my mother aspired to a high-toned Catholicism, big on ritual, short on hysteria. Her Irish identity expressed itself in a passionate affair with language, believing perhaps far too blindly in the power of the right word or phrase to carry the day, the month, even the years. My mother would likely not have approved of this synopsis. She did not relish it if I disparaged my roots, transmogrifying into a banshee whenever she suspected that I had failed to give my Irish American heritage its proper shine. We grew up hearing stories of discrimination and cruelty, including one about the hanging of two young Irishmen in Northampton, Massachusetts, in the nineteenth century whose crime was being in the wrong place at the wrong time. "Do not ever," she said, "act like an obsequious peasant." And then she would add, "Even in the worst of times we have always had people of consequence in our lineage. We can always summon the cousin who went to Yale, not to mention that distant relative who invented the submarine." At the time she made this comment, she was ninety-two years old, and I ignored the scold in her words in favor of their cadence. It is a pearl necklace of a sentence, elegant and understated. As such it adds credence to my conviction that one of the ways in which John's and my family could not be more alike is that both are brimful of people who live by language—lawyers, editors, writers, teachers, therapists. The second bond is that the two families share a passion for politics with a strong nod to social justice. We worshipped the Kennedys; they knew them.

When John first met my family in 1976 or so, we were gathered, my sibs and some of their friends, in the living room of a cottage on Sound Breeze Avenue in Groton Long Point, Connecticut, that belonged to my uncle, Dermot Purcell Shea, my mother's brother who did his best to be an auxiliary parent. I don't remember an adult being present. My sister Christina's then husband, Bob, was strumming a guitar, and all of us were decked out in the uniform of the day (patched jeans, flannel shirts, bandannas). My sister Jacqueline, always given to whimsy, was arguing that her goal of being a "happy-go-lucky Sylvia Plath" made sense. Smoke from various strains of tobacco swirled around the room—a tame 1970s scene compared with "the center is not holding" mood of the era, a time of dropouts and runaways among the young. My family could be seen as almost conservative in that light. No ashrams or communes or self-actualizing vision quests for us. With the exception of my older brother, Raymond, who was ill and unable to finish high school, the rest of us were dedicated to getting a college degree from either public universities or Catholic women's colleges in a timely fashion, our tuition paid for by loans, government grants, work-study, and scholarships.

No one even noticed John for about a half an hour.

Finally, either my youngest sister, Maureen, the patient and empathic special education teacher, or my younger brother, Michael, then a student at Rutgers in Camden, said, "Who's he?"

I remember the look on John's face, the look of freedom dawning: *This is cool. These people barely take attendance.* His childhood in rarefied Washington circles was followed by four years as an adolescent in what he calls a maximum-security prison, which is to say he went to a prep school whose name he does not utter to this day. For John, my family must have been a relief from the pressures of the exalted expectations built into his background: the pack of kids, the anonymity, the lack of formal introductions. Who's he, indeed.

I had met John's parents at around the same time at a dinner at Café des Artistes in New York City. The evening passed in a blur of mutual courtesies. Eager as I was for a broader canvas, I noted, with approval, that Nick and Lydia Katzenbach made sophisticated dining choices, involving hazelnuts and organ meats and saffron, though not all at once of course. As if I understood the first thing about fine dining: at the time I was trying to remember whether "bisque" had one syllable or two, and I never could keep it straight whether "fillet" applied to fish or meat or both. My family was the opposite of food snobs. There was no such thing as gourmet. We were the perfect market segment for family packs, for brown tuna, and for Tang. My childhood meals stood out mostly for how quickly we ate, every night at six p.m., after *The Mickey Mouse Club* and before *Bonanza*, and my mother's continual exhortations: "Be grateful. Don't choke."

I knew that John's father had served in the Kennedy and Johnson administrations, including as undersecretary of state, as assistant attorney general, and as attorney general. I expected the nation's former top lawyer to be intimidating, but he was soft-spoken and mild-mannered. Lydia, on the other hand, was formidable. Feminism was sweeping the nation, but one still didn't find many women with such swagger. She was finishing her training to become a lay (meaning extensive training, but no medical degree) psychoanalyst, a shrink—a midlife career change from full-time wife, mother, and hostess. My family prided itself on knowing doctors, but they all dealt with the concrete—feet, teeth, insides— nothing so phantasmagoric as the psyche.

Our diverse backgrounds were clearly part of the attraction. John is from what used to be called a "prominent family," meaning that most members had attained a certain level of accomplishment and high regard after a suitably long tenure in America, the kind of family where one might find headmasters, bishops, and bankers. In their case, the lineage included the inventor of most of the international laws for yachting (I can hear John's brother, Chris the lawyer, asking, "What's wrong? Why not all?"). They also claimed the occasional Bolshevik and madman and Revolutionary War soldier. This last was a fellow who got the British troops drunk on the night before Washington's crossing of the Delaware, so he was either a hero or a traitor depending on which side you were on.

When John asked me if I wanted to visit his family's *shack* on Martha's Vineyard one day during the summer of 1976, my first thought was relief that someone in Trenton had even heard of Martha's Vineyard. I have pride of place, and the Garden State was getting to me. New Jersey, after all, names toilets on the turnpike after poets. It has gangsters in the landfill. And that accent:

"worter" for "water" and "over deir" for "over there" and "collitch" for "college."

I had been to Martha's Vineyard several times before his invitation, during an interlude in my career when I was not giving voice to the voiceless but rather covering the posh and the powerful at the Boston bureau of *Women's Wear Daily*. If you are ever at a loss for conversation on Martha's Vineyard, just start talking about your first experience of the island. It's contagious: soon everyone else is talking about theirs. Watch as eyes glaze over in a grateful retrieval of some remembered happiness, neat and rectangular as a postcard: the honor system custom of leaving your shoes at the entrance to Lucy Vincent Beach, the sunset in Menemsha, or the smell of bread at the farmers' market.

Two postcards, then.

Postcard #1

The first is from July 1973. *WWD* assigned me to cover a book party. The island was new to me, despite its long history as a port of call and fishing power and as home to the Wampanoag Native American tribe. The celebration honored Anne Simon's *No Island Is an Island*, in which she showed her support for Ted Kennedy's Islands Trust Bill, known simply as the Kennedy Bill, intended to save Martha's Vineyard from developers. It would have taken the future of the island out of the hands of the locals and placed it with the feds.

Women in summer cottons floated by. Men open-shirted, tan, puffing, as was the custom in those days, on cigarettes. The template for this gathering—accomplished people toasting one another on accomplishments with white wine and witticisms—endures on the island to this day, but I did not know that then. All I knew was that everyone appeared to possess private radar for one another's pedigree, and I struggled to record the names of people pointed out as heavy hitters, which was just about everybody at the event, including the social scientist Vance Packard, biographer David McCullough, historian Barbara Tuchman, and William Styron, perhaps the best novelist of his generation. An older fellow named Henry Beetle Hough, who was against more people and more buildings, kept repeating the same quip: "This bill will do for the island what the pill has done for the rest of the world's population. Save it. I'm for the bill and the pill." Hough, I was told, was the longtime editor of the *Vineyard Gazette*, who retired and was replaced in 1967 by James "Scotty" Reston of the *New York Times*.

Those who favored home rule opposed the bill: "The bill is an example of the thirties, with the so-called enlightened federal government taking control of the island's future out of the five thousand year-round residents," one partygoer said.

The singer Carly Simon, three months pregnant, with a tall, crusading air and long hair framing her generous features, was in favor of government restrictions, the sooner the better: "Why, there was a traffic jam, a real traffic jam. In Vineyard Haven! This afternoon!" she said as I scribbled in my notebook, giving this offhand comment the weight of an edict.

Her brother, Peter, kept snapping her photo. Her husband at the time, James Taylor, didn't show up: "It's not his scene."

I didn't care. Carly Simon was probably the foremost female vocal artist of the day. All I could think was: *Wait till I tell my friends I interviewed the "You're So Vain" girl.*

That story was a quick in and out. Like hundreds of thousands of new visitors, I couldn't evict the island from my mind, vowing to return if the chance ever arose.

Postcard #2

I developed a better sense of the island when I came back not much later with a photographer, this time to interview Scotty Reston and his wife, Sally (sometimes referred to as "my girl Sally" by her husband), during the thick of the Watergate hearings. He was considered a god of rational discourse at the time, and the editors at *WWD* made their opinion of him clear in a large-font all-caps headline: "AMERICA'S CONSCIENCE."

For the interview, the Restons wore matching blue Mao jackets from a recent trip to China, 100 percent natural fabric with plenty of pockets.

"Why, when Sally and I were young, sometimes we'd just spend long hours reading to each other. It was a way, really, of making love," he revealed, before engaging on the topic of the *Gazette*. "The paper has total absorption of the island homes," he said, "but it's a publication with limited advertising potential."

"The paper makes friends, not money," she said.

Like the *Times*, he said the *Gazette* was a paper of record: "The biggest difference is that inaccuracy is a personalized problem and you're liable to get a punch in the nose if you misquote someone."

As for John's invitation to visit the island, I was twenty-eight, not so young that I still thought of the future as an endless bolt of luxuriant fabric, but still eager to be seen as footloose and spontaneous. Sure, the Vineyard. Why not?

As for "shack," I dismissed the term as one of those Protestant pet names, a class-conscious toning down of a seaside compound complete with guesthouses and servants' quarters, maybe even a pool and tennis courts. John planned on being a novelist, and I assumed he was practicing the art of invention on me, a kind of harmless recreational lying.

"Very rustic and down-to-earth," he said, persisting on his track of lowering all expectations. "No electricity. Just a hand pump at the sink. You don't mind mice? Outhouse. Outdoor shower."

We made plans to visit the island when I would have a few days off following the Democratic National Convention, held in Madison Square Garden in 1976, a spectacle that ended up with the nomination of Jimmy Carter for president of the United States.

I remembered Lydia from our previous dinner and I tried to picture her in a camp-like setting. I had personally witnessed, and praised, her high heels; admired her apricot-colored hair, arranged in a stunning updo that clearly depended on a complex orchestration of hair dryers and sprays and mirrors; and observed her fabulous long fingers and her beautiful nails. Not exactly hand pump at the sink material. Even with my limited knowledge from that one encounter, I could not imagine her in anything less than a well-appointed setting.

No way John's family had a *shack*.

Still, I was eager to accept the invitation.

And so, on the road to Martha's Vineyard from New Jersey that first time, John continued to lower my expectations. "I should warn you. Nothing fancy. My dad's not big on home repair. The house is kind of falling apart. The roof is leaking so he tacked up these green garbage bags on the ceiling . . ."

Okay.

"After a hard rain, the bags burst and, well, there's this brown ooze."

Ooze?

The house was either a science fair experiment gone awry, or . . . John was lying. I went with lying.

The more he hinted at squalor, the more I imagined the opposite. I remembered something else from my dinner with his parents, how his mother said they lived in Riverdale, New York, in a house on the Hudson River. She said it looked like a castle, and when her own mother first saw it, she turned to Lydia and said, "It's just wonderful, dear, but do you really need a moat?"

The house in Riverdale had ghosts, one of which was as good as it gets in the ghost department: a jilted bride rumored to sweep in and out of otherwise unoccupied rooms on the third floor, keening as she went, a cloud of tearful embittered white.

One of the rooms on the first floor with a view of the river was pronounced to have perfect acoustics by no less a personage than Toscanini.

Naturally, I packed all the necessities, including a nifty portable travel iron for pressing summer linens.

We buzzed up Interstate 95 in the red Datsun 240Z, reliable or not, radio blaring. Jimmy Carter was on a campaign swing through the southern states, Hank Aaron hit a home run, and some legionnaires at a convention in Philadelphia were suffering from an outbreak of a mystery disease. The radio kept playing the same song: "Don't Go Breaking My Heart" by Elton John.

"Assuming no traffic," John said, "we should be there in under four hours."

Factored into the timetable was the irritating necessity of stopping what seemed like every two minutes in Connecticut to throw quarters into bins, back when it was the Toll Booth State. We headed north into Rhode Island and toward Massachusetts, edging past Fall River and New Bedford, past Lizzie Borden and shoe factories. Then the Bourne Bridge, with the large sign pleading against suicide and a dramatic plummeting view of the Cape Cod Canal. Down Route 28—past a go-cart place, shingled houses close to the road, gas stations that advertised lobster rolls along with air for your tires—toward Woods Hole and the ferry.

At Woods Hole, as long as you weren't blocking someone's driveway or too close to a fire hydrant, you could leave your car willy-nilly and you could toss your suitcase on a luggage trolley to send on its own to the other side: no IDs required, no inquiries from the feds. Today, the large, cumbersome, ungainly, and lurching ferries take forty-five minutes or so to get from Woods Hole to their two ports of call, Vineyard Haven and Oak Bluffs. Each houses a lackluster snack bar with chowder, beer, and ancient wrinkled hot dogs. Upon departure, a blast of the foghorn and garbled words of welcome over the loudspeaker:

"This is a smoke-free vessel. No luggage on the seats. No dogs on seats. All animals on a leash. No animals in the lunch counter area. Thanks for traveling on the Steamship Authority. Have a pleasant day."

The guys who work the boat speak in eastern Massachusetts accents, which entail adding Rs or omitting them, but rarely using the correct amount in the normal place. They project the hardiness of people you can trust with heavy machinery and who you assume must have hated sitting still in a classroom.

If you are lucky and the traffic is light and the ferry is punctual, the ride will offer you, in a remarkably short amount of time, an excellent transition. The minute you let the air wash over you on the deck, you can feel yourself beginning to detox from winter and scaly skin and scheduled expectations. As for summer, I have a native New Englander's admiration for the sun of summer, its gloating triumph. Even in frigid weather, summer sells: I remember a display window at a jewelry store in Boston in January with necklaces draped around ice-cream cones. Folklore, if not fact, indicates that Massachusetts has more ice-cream opportunities than any other place in the nation and that wintertime consumption is as high as in the summer, perhaps in the melting, luscious hope of summoning an eighty-degree day. John always says that the governor of the Commonwealth should have just one job: to let people know all the sunny temperate days on the first of the year so they can plan accordingly. Even hospitals have to take the local love of summer into account. Most elective surgery is scheduled during the winter months. Come summer, no one wants to give up a single backyard barbecue.

For that first trip together, I toted a backpack, canvas with leather straps, from L.L.Bean. It had accompanied me all the way to Europe, *the* Europe, as I liked to say. After we arrived on the island in Vineyard Haven, we stuck our thumbs out and hitched seven or eight miles south across its belly, then headed west past the main airport, past a farm or two, past a place that sold wildflowers in coffee cans and had a sign for pony-riding lessons. Cars—mostly dirt-streaked and dented station wagons—stopped readily, with no concerns about potential foul play on either side of the equation. When John suddenly asked to be let off on the side of a dirt road that resembled any number of dirt roads we had just gone by, I had no faith that this patch of sand was any more likely to be the correct one than the patch of sand just before it, or the one just after, but he exuded confidence and I followed.

Deep Bottom Road proved to be a series of disconcerting bumps and dips. John said some years were worse than others depending on the severity of the rainfall. Clearly it had rained recently. A lot.

We walked a mile, winding our way past little dirt road tributaries through dense forest. Another mile, now straight and muddy and a little less narrow. Along the way, trees sometimes featured little homemade signs with a name or initials, indicating a house hidden in the distance.

"Not much more to go," John kept reassuring me, the road now curving to hug a pond on the left. I still expected that after our trudge there would arise from the mists a glorious edifice replete with all the accoutrements of civilization, including running water and a fully operational roof.

What I finally saw was a . . . shack, three or four rooms the size of big closets hammered to one another without any architectural forethought. John said it had been built at the turn of the twentieth century for the mistress of a well-to-do sea captain in Edgartown, endowing the place with a sense of the illicit, which thrilled his mom, who apparently liked drama and bad behavior, who cottoned to the notion of a randy sailor and his ethereal mermaid. (I am not so sure about this story. The pond is on the eastern flyway for migrant waterfowl. The geese and ducks are so plentiful that in the early 1900s, hunters built shacks with stoves so they could wait for their prey to arrive from Canada in comfort.

But a lone guy waiting to kill birds isn't as romantic as Lydia's vision of passionate assignations, so I'm going with the mistress/captain version.)

I was less easily enamored.

Having grown up in an old center-staircase Colonial built in 1790, I had had my fill of the style in which charm routs efficiency at every turn.

I'd done Girl Scout camp, done communal living in primitive circumstances.

I had experienced student-style poverty and had recently practiced the prim economies of someone fresh to the workforce paying back student loans.

It was then that I got an inkling of how some people delight in deprivation, even court it. The idea of a certain kind of cheerful self-abnegation in gorgeous settings was new to me, the notion that patched elbows, fraying hems, and chipped dishes throw perfect vistas into relief and also the notion that the less your summer setting resembled the heavy baggage of your winter setting, the better.

I drank in my environs with a wary glance.

The ceiling was indeed covered with green garbage bags to catch the rain that sometimes leaked through the shingles. The windows had masking tape slashed across them as protection against a long-ago hurricane, big Xs, giving the mistaken impression that at some point there had been a quarantine. Mice had what appeared to be major mice get-togethers in every room at all hours, and the hand pump was as temperamental as a sleep-deprived teenager. Many years later John confessed to me something I have decided is not true: that once when he opened the house after a long winter, he felt something hard and petrified inside a pillow. He says it was a rat, though he could have just as easily, and with a greater sense of decency, called it a squirrel.

Scrunched up on a tiny window seat, I stared out at the low-lying vegetation known as broom—fat shrubs with slender branches, tiny leaves, and yellow flowers—and consoled myself that at least the air was bracing.

Did it take an entire day or just mere hours to finally get into the rhythm of the place?

I could even envision Lydia here, if only for a few days at a time.

Soon, I saw the house in a different light.

It felt fey, like a toy dwelling, the kind you might find in a Margaret Wise Brown picture book about a house that belonged to itself with a view from a bluff that was more than enough.

It didn't take long to see everything with a more forgiving gaze.

The shower connected to a tree that was gnarled and spindly, the perfect tree for the job. Its limbs moved every which way, as if they were in a constant process of soaping themselves.

The shack was on a tidal pond, leading to the ocean.

The world was in layers—the blue gray of the pond, the beige lip of sand in the distance, the different blue of the ocean, and yet another blue for the sky—an orgy of horizons, interrupted now and then by white birds, white foam, and white clouds.

The pond itself was well stocked with oysters and crabs, which provided cheap eats for guests with a can-do scavenging streak. The shack was located among what is reputed to be one of the best huckleberry patches on the island.

You could haul in groceries, or you could forage.

Being beneath all that sky and next to all that water had a lulling effect. The location of the shack proved addictive in the sense that it blotted out all other realities.

Why not forage?

After a few days by the pond you became a happy animal, scampering barefoot, feral, and fortified.

How had John's family ever found this place? In the tried-and-true tradition, first coming to the island as renters, falling in love, and dreaming of a more permanent relationship.

John remembers visits from when he was ten; before then the family spent its vacations on Pearl Island in Upper Saint Regis Lake in the Adirondacks.

"The first time we stayed at Quenames, a renovated farmhouse that was near the Quenames Road that runs to Black Point Beach. A couple of summers—it was really rustic. That was where I found and tried to train a wild hawk named Squawk. He would ride on my shoulder and sometimes on the handlebars. Very sad for a ten-year-old—he died—I think he ate something wrong. Don't know. We drove hell for leather to the vet hospital but they couldn't save him. Never could figure out the cause—we fed him lots and he was capable of flying off and then returning. I sometimes wonder whether there wasn't something nefarious at work.

"Next to Quenames one of the Whitings (Everett, I think) had a sheep farm. Lots of sheep in the area. On shearing day, Rocky, our Great Pyrenees, was incredibly excited, racing about, watching the farmers bring in the sheep and watching them cut the wool. She was zooming up and down past a six-foot fence that bordered the property. Suddenly, one of the sheep broke free and took off

36

in fifth gear across the field. Too much for Rocky, who had never seen a sheep before in her life. She went over the fence, chased the wayward sheep down, and drove it all the way back into the barn. Legend has it that Ev Whiting offered my dad a thousand dollars for her on the spot. He turned it down.

"We also stayed at Ed Logue's house—Stilt House—just off South Road on Chilmark Pond. Ed was a prominent Bostonian, an architect and very famous. We were there for August several summers. I liked it because it was close to Vernon Eagle's house."

Vernon Eagle (father of Sioux, a well-known jeweler with a shop in Vineyard Haven) had been a longtime friend of the Katzenbachs'. He and Nick both taught at the University of Chicago in the 1950s. John's favorite story about Vernon: "At the age of twenty-four, Vernon Eagle lost a leg while serving with the British Commandos in North Africa fighting against [General Erwin] Rommel. At a cocktail party in London early in 1945, in full dress, he listened as a British woman complained about how weary she was of the rationing. Hadn't they all sacrificed enough? Vernon sidled over to a buffet table, where he grabbed a sterling silver pick from an ice bucket. He then returned to the woman and placed himself in her direct line of vision, plunging the device into his prosthesis, *wham*. He didn't say a word about sacrifice. Didn't have to."

In a coincidence that would make bad fiction, but works in life, I had a photo of Vernon in my possession when I moved to Trenton. I did not know them, but a friend had taken a black-and-white picture of Vernon striding one-legged on his crutches, on the beach, to where a beautiful young woman, his other daughter Mary, stretched out in the sand. Everything about the photo, its composition, its subtext, the incongruity of forms, spoke to me. I framed it in bright yellow, the color of sunshine and candor, the minute I got it, and it has been in every house I have lived in ever since.

"Also, we stayed at the Wisniewski House, which was famous, as the prominent architect had designed it with all glass walls. It was down toward Menemsha. I think I was about fifteen by then. Anyway, the house was a mess: no insulation, so when the temp dropped at night you would have to pile on the blankets. But as soon as the sun rose, all the rooms would boil. The house was a rectangle, with an inner walkway surrounding a garden linking all the rooms. When we arrived, there were big Xs in red tape on every sliding door. My mother, naturally, thought these aesthetically not pleasing, so she removed all of them. That night, my father got a two a.m. call from the White House. I can still remember the sound of her feet on the walkway as she ran to answer the phone in the living room—and the *thud!* when she crashed into the sliding door that you couldn't see because the Xs had been removed. This was also the house where antiwar protesters stuck a sign in front one day while we were at the beach. Seems tame now.

"Finally, we spent some summers at what was called the Gun Club out on Tisbury Great Pond. It's the place operated by the Trustees of Reservations now. It was a shooting lodge—there used to be duck and geese blinds all over the pond for the fall hunting season. That would offend many sensibilities today. Lots of stuffed animals on the walls. But you could walk to the beach . . .

"I think it was the summers at the Gun Club—and visiting Tony and Linda Lewis at their place—that persuaded my folks that the pond was where they wanted to be."

The Lewis camp, a few doors down from the shack, hidden from view, frequently enticed its visitors to dream of becoming owners. Anthony Lewis was a columnist for the *New York Times* and a recipient of two Pulitzer Prizes. Linda Lewis, his wife at the time, and the mother of his three children, was a writer and a dancer. They lived in Cambridge in the winter and radiated 02138: intimacy with Harvard and with *Masterpiece Theatre*, a global consciousness especially in regard to England and Africa, and a high degree of literacy. I remember Linda announcing one summer that she planned to *reread* (not read) all of Trollope. On the island, she gave dinner parties that not only featured playwright Lillian Hellman's bluefish recipe, but also Lillian Hellman herself. (The secret is dried mustard.)

The land and the shack were purchased in the early 1970s for what was considered an exorbitant sum of $80,000, causing neighbors to pity the Katzenbachs for their wanton ways. By 1978, two years after my first visit, the shack was gone, transformed into rubble and memory. The Katzenbachs built a bigger house in its place, still a simple structure, but more sturdy. Once again, no basement and no heat, except from a fireplace in the living room and a gas stove in one of the bedrooms. The house was usable, depending on one's level of hardiness, for about six months of the year.

The zoning authorities mandated a setback of one hundred feet from the high-water mark. From across the pond a vigilant neighbor was convinced that the house was a foot closer to the water than the legal requirements specified, but when he visited the property and saw its purposeful modesty up close, he withdrew his objection. The house, one story tall, melded into the landscape so that from the beach it was barely visible, an architectural courtesy deeply appreciated by the neighbors.

It helped that the builder, Donald DeSorcy, enjoyed universal respect on the island, and the glow extended to the people lucky enough to hire him. When DeSorcy died at the start of our final summer, island attorney Ron Rappaport offered several anecdotes that captured his style in the *Gazette*:

> Approximately 30 years ago, a friend of mine asked me to recommend the best builder on the Vineyard and I recommended Donald. After viewing his work, my friend and his architect came to the same conclusion. We set up a meeting with Donald to work out a contract. Donald simply said, "I don't do contracts. You are just going to have to trust me." After a closed-door meeting, my friend, an experienced businessman, shook Donald's hand and said, "Okay, I've never done business this way before, but I trust you. Build me a house." Donald told him the house would be done the following November.
>
> Sometime during the spring, my friend came to inspect the house and we had another meeting with Donald. My friend said to Donald: "I'll pay you an extra $50,000 if the house can be ready by July 1." Donald sat there for the longest time, didn't say anything, thought about it, and then just said, "Nope." There was no negotiation, no counter offer. Nothing. Just, "Nope." My friend said he had never seen anybody take such a blunt, unyielding position without trying to negotiate something else. But that is the way Donald was. Blunt, straightforward and honest.
>
> On another occasion, Donald was asked to do a major renovation of a house in West Tisbury. When he walked in to meet the potential customers, he was asked to

take off his shoes before he could enter the house. Donald looked around and said: "This job isn't going to work out." And he turned around and left.

The only problem with the new house was its very newness. It was not the stuff of legend like the shack, not mired in rumors of embezzled embraces. John and I devised a plan to create our own mythology. We ordered actual ship's logs from an outfit in Maine in which you could have the name of your vessel printed on the beige cover. Instead, we customized the title of each book to suit our purposes as a way to record our time on the island: first "Summer Notes," then "Son of Summer Notes" and "The Unending Summer Notes" and "The Return of the Summer Notes," a theme we later discarded in favor of less predictable, less buttoned-down titles. It took a while, a few years in fact, for the first one to fill up, but as soon as it did, a clamor for successors followed. The logs, which began as a routine gift, as much for us as anyone else, ended up as prized possessions. They were, for most everyone, the first item new arrivals sought out, lunging after them like gulls to crumbs, and writing in them was the last task, the final ritual, the blowing out of a kind of a candle, before leaving.

Chapter Three

Turn Right, Turn Left

Finding your way around Martha's Vineyard is not an easy task, because no one on the island gives normal directions. First of all, the actual names of streets are rarely used. Instead, you will be told to take "the road that goes from Alley's toward Chilmark" or "the one where they have that road race." Next a jumble of orders: "Travel 2.7 miles and turn right when you see four mailboxes—four, not six—and after three dips in the road—three, not two—turn right at the fork and take your next left."

I mentioned how during one of my first visits to the island I got to interview Scotty and Sally Reston. What I did not say is that after our formal Q&A, I experienced one of those moments as a reporter when you can't believe your good fortune.

The Restons offered the photographer and me a tour of the island.

First, Edgartown Harbor for a quick spin in their small motorboat.

"No sailboats for us," he said. "We're both from the Midwest and far too lubberly for that." Back on land he pointed out some gullies where "in the fall the barberry bushes turn to crimson and bronze. There are great valleys of those things. And people wonder why we come here."

We circumnavigated the island by car, winding up at Cedar Tree Neck Sanctuary, a four-hundred-acre preserve where a sign forbade fishing, swimming, biking, and picnicking.

"All you can do is stare," said Scotty. "And that is entertainment enough."

Could either he or his wife remember what initially attracted them to the island?

She said, after a pause, "The beauty and the quiet, I guess."

"Maybe it's the melody of the place," he added.

The beauty and the quiet and the melody.

Since that day, I have circled the island many times, leading tours for others as the Restons once did for me—minus the quick spin on the harbor. Often, I recite the logistical boilerplate pretty much word for word: "Martha's Vineyard is approximately 96 square miles, roughly triangular in shape, 25 miles at its longest point east to west, and 9 miles at the longest point north to south."

On the tours, I would give a quick history lesson: the original inhabitants, the Wampanoags, living in Aquinnah ("land under the hill"), called the island Noepe ("land amid the water"), but in 1602, an English explorer named Bartholomew Gosnold arrived and quickly renamed the island Martha after his daughter or his wife—the accounts vary—and "Vineyard" for the wild grapes on the island. He renamed Aquinnah "Gay Head" after the stunning colors on the clay cliffs. Forty years later a Massachusetts man named Thomas Mayhew purchased the island as well as Nantucket and the Elizabeth Islands from two Englishmen, who claimed ownership. He paid forty pounds. Up until the Civil War the island was a major player in the whaling industry. Afterward, it slowly but surely built up a clientele of summer visitors so that tourism is now the chief industry.

I would also explain that there are six towns—Tisbury, Oak Bluffs, Edgartown, West Tisbury, Chilmark, and Aquinnah—and each one is different, but they have one element in common, which speaks to an implicit regard on the island for literacy and literature: they all have a library.

The name of our street was confusing. Deep Bottom Road is often changed to Deep Bottom Cove Road because it is on Deep Bottom Cove. No matter what you call it, it dead-ends at what we called the "main road," where we had to make a decision: turn right, turn left. It always felt like a political choice. Left meant the scenic route, toward West Tisbury and beyond. The speed limit on this road (whatever its name) quickly diminishes to 20 mph. We always assumed this was the one sure way the West Tisbury Police Department figured out to balance its budget. Right meant we would be headed to one of the "cities," toward Edgartown, Oak Bluffs, or Vineyard Haven, where you found the majority of the island's stores and restaurants.

A sweep of the island reveals low-lying trees, dunes, working farms, windmills, fishing docks, hidden beaches, bait shops, and pie stands. The island has five elementary schools, a charter school and a high school, a hospital and two airports (one so small it doesn't really count). It has at least one dirt road whose official name is Dirt Road and a street called Driveway with two houses on it. Unlike Nantucket, which is smaller and was once a barrier island and so is even more vulnerable to the elements, the Vineyard was formerly a part of the mainland millennia ago, giving the Vineyard a geological edge in terms of its survival and also providing the source of yet another little interisland jab. The allegiance is such that some families require newcomers to take a loyalty oath. When the writer Richard Russo's daughter Emily was married, he told an interviewer that her sister, Kate, as the maid of honor, gave "this hilarious talk called 'Russos for Dummies' welcoming Steve into the family," telling him there were certain things he had to do to be a Russo.

"And one of them was you had to love Martha's Vineyard in order to be welcomed. We just couldn't imagine anybody coming into this family that didn't like it. Or that preferred Nantucket."

The place names on the island (Squibnocket, Lobsterville, Tashmoo, Takemmy, East Chop, West Chop, Quenames, Moshup Trail) play games with your head, teasing fake definitions from the sounds themselves. Edgartown could be a scary theme park based on stories by Poe. Oak Bluffs, a strategy in poker. Chilmark, a mean minister in a Hawthorne novel, and Tisbury ('tis berry), a quaint way to describe the inside of a pie.

Menemsha: a word that people love to pronounce and to guess at its meaning. When I first heard it, I wanted it to be my pseudonym, not that I actually needed one. Someone once said it sounds like a Jewish holiday.

John's sister Mimi, in an essay called "Parachute" that she wrote for photographer Peter Simon's collection entitled *On the Vineyard*, described Menemsha as "the word a woman, opening her arms, says to a man."

On my tours, we usually turned left at the main road so we could travel first through West Tisbury: a maze of dirt roads and secret ponds, and an art mecca, with an outdoor sculpture museum across from Alley's, short for Alley's General Store, with its sign: IF YOU DON'T SEE IT ASK FOR IT. Established in 1858, it is a store that claims, somewhat correctly, to be "dealers in almost everything." Inside, a panoply of random items: canned peas, fertilizer, kerosene, Hula-Hoops, towels, lobster placemats, glasses, American flags, penny candy, Wiffle balls, boogie boards, and, of course, newspapers.

Up the street from Alley's is Grange Hall, which hosts a farmers' market on Wednesdays and Saturdays in high season and a craft market on Thursdays and Sundays. A sarong skirt with a pleasing drape costs ninety dollars on July 31 and one hundred on August 1, a reflection of the sentiment that August is prime time on the island, with higher rents and even wealthier visitors.

If my guests were feeling flush, we might detour to the Granary Gallery on Old County Road, with paintings by several dozen artists including Kib Bramhall, Ray Ellis, Barbara Day, Mary Sipp Green, and Allen Whiting.

Land by water is always about light, and light always attracts artists. And photographers, also featured at the Granary. Alfred Eisenstaedt summered on the island. Famous as one of four original photographers for *Life* magazine and as a National Medal of Arts award recipient, he took the photo of the sailor kissing the girl titled

V-J Day in Times Square in 1945. When John's father retired from the board of the Washington Post Company, Katharine Graham, the former publisher, arranged for photographer Alison Shaw to shoot the house at Thumb Point as a private commission. Shaw remembers racing down Deep Bottom Road, up the main road, and then down another long dirt road to catch the sun in the evening from two different angles. Every summer, one of our rituals was to visit the Granary Gallery in West Tisbury and to pine after her work. From time to time, we indulged our desires and now have her images of boats, clouds, decks, water, and palette knives throughout our house.

Usually we saved the gallery for a special trip and continued heading up-island toward Chilmark. No matter how often I remind myself that soon the ocean will surge into view, the sight of the water is always stunning, as satisfying and theatrical as when a gun goes off in the third act of a play.

In Chilmark you pass Abel's Hill Cemetery where Blues Brother John Belushi is buried: tour buses pay their respects during the season. On the other side of the road, the Allen farm (formal name: the Allen Farm Sheep and Wool Company) provides a wedding venue par excellence: the price was $17,000 to rent for a week in June 2016. The venue has lodgings so wedding guests can rent rooms on the property, substantially lowering the actual cost for the hosts. One of the quirks of getting married there is that female guests are advised to wear flat or low-heeled shoes due to the squishiness of the landscape.

Farther down is the Chilmark Community Center, which in season causes almost as many traffic jams as an arriving ferry. It is a well-used building, with a morning program for children in July and August and summer evening presentations, including earnest panel discussions, such as one on menopause, "Still Doing It: The Intimate Lives of Women over 65." Lectures and more lectures: Would summer on the island really be summer if First Amendment lawyer Alan Dershowitz did not opine in front of an audience on topics such as the legal battles that transformed our nation? Or environmentalists on the movement to restore the heath hen, described by the *Gazette* as no less than the "gateway bird for de-extinction"? Or Ward Just reading from one of his novels, his gravelly voice taking his audience to Africa or Vietnam or Berlin?

Then you arrive at Beetlebung Corner.

Three choices:

You can go left, taking you to Moshup Trail, but first you pass the Chilmark General Store, which claims that "whether you're making a pit stop or stocking your pantry for a week we have grocery basics covered: from Coca-Cola to Kombucha, we strive to find a balance between convenience and inspiration." Kombucha, that famous kitchen staple. The store's wide porch, with its armada of rocking chairs, fills up all summer with people who may or may not be famous, bike riders in need of a pit stop, children from the nearby camp when it gets out at noon, as well as a perennial supply of earnest little boys explaining in their scariest voices to anyone who will listen about the different kinds of sharks in the water and why you don't want any of them to mistake you for a seal. You will also pass Chilmark Chocolates (open only sometimes). Menemsha Pond will be on your right. The final destination is Aquinnah: the lighthouse, clay cliffs, sacred burial grounds. During the high season, buses disgorge tourists as they elbow their way past the gift shops and clam shacks to the views. It has the most remote location and, as a result, possesses the glamour of a recluse. The lighthouse is a premier proposal site and the Outermost Inn, owned by Hugh Taylor of the Simon-Taylor dynasty, a premier honeymoon spot. Aquinnah is where Jackie Kennedy Onassis had her estate. A blog from one of her maids describes the former First Lady's days as simple. Breakfast of bran, skim milk, and fruit. Lunch of carrots and cottage cheese and iced tea. She swam two hours a day in Squibnocket Pond. Dinner: fish or meat, salad, a glass of wine. And she required a fire in her bedroom fireplace no matter what the weather.

Second, you can go (sort of) straight and you will wind down a pretty road with tucked-away hotels and pricey restaurants and a classic white church before happening upon Menemsha, a fishing village within the town of Chilmark, timeless and melancholy, especially at sunset with boats bobbing off of dark docks near the faded Texaco gas station where you expect to find Moxie or sarsaparilla floating in ice in a metal chest for a nickel a bottle. You can easily imagine the scene as a painting by Hopper: *Texaco at Menemsha at Twilight.*

Two fish markets compete with each other here, Larsen's and an establishment often referred to as the Place That Used to Be Called Poole's, named after its former owners, Everett Poole, with his craggy face and ever-present pipe, and his son, Donald. Pandora's Box sells women's clothing. Across the street, the Bite, a fried seafood joint where the words "Atkins" and "carbohydrates" have likely never been uttered, except perhaps as expletives.

Or third, you can take a sharp right and you will be on "the road that takes you to North Road," also known as oh-so-hilly

Middle Street, where I idled away many a summer day at a flea market eyeing charm bracelets, which may or may not be antique, for seventy-five dollars, along with cotton bandannas for seven, painted canvas rugs, maps, beaded jewelry, pocketbooks and pillows made out of faintly faded vintage fabric, straw hats, used jeans in mint condition, and teacups. You can buy a samovar or a wicker table or a wastebasket decorated in laminate with headlines, such as the one that said "YES!!!" from the *Boston Globe* after the Red Sox won the 2004 World Series.

Beetlebung Corner, another memorable Vineyard name, often sparks curiosity as to its origin. If asked, I am likely to explain that Beetlebungs are trees related to dogwoods. John is likely to ignore matters of etymology in favor of recounting a teenaged memory: "My best friend, Craigie, wanted to drive the 1958 black Volkswagen Beetle that was my brother's and my first car."

Craigie, John's childhood friend from D.C., is Craig McNamara, son of Robert McNamara, secretary of defense during the Vietnam War. Robert McNamara was the first president of Ford Motor Company outside of the Ford family and is considered one of the primary forces behind seat belts, well before the government demanded them as standard equipment. His tenure was short, recruited early on by John Kennedy to serve in his administration. McNamara was a math whiz who took his numbers game to the war in Vietnam and was blamed for much of its escalation. Eventually Craig would grow up to be a walnut farmer in California, a gentle can-do guy said by his wife to possess the "chipper gene," but at this moment long ago, in John's memory, he is just a kid who hasn't quite mastered the art of steering.

John's version of their terrifying ride:

"No seat belts. No gas gauge. Four speeds and sixty horse-power. This car had once belonged to a Catholic clergyman. On the dashboard there was a sign that said: IN THE EVENT OF AN ACCIDENT, CALL A PRIEST.

"Anyway, we took off for Gay Head (to see some girls) on a night filled with spectacular fog. Fog like gray mud in front of the windscreen. Fog so thick, visibility was perhaps ten feet.

"Before the Chilmark Store or the police station or the library or anything else at Beetlebung Corner, including the stop signs, there was only an old church with a beautiful stone wall in front. Gone now.

"So, in the fog, inexperienced driver Craigie missed the turn. Significantly. All of a sudden, we're bouncing along on the dirt and lawn belonging to the old church. Craig spins the wheel when I yell. The only thing I can see in the fog is a telephone pole.

"We miss it.

"Lots of teenage laughter. Down the road to see the girls.

"Went back the next day, wondering how close we'd come.

"Our front tire track was six inches from the pole and the stone wall. That meant we'd missed it by an inch. Maybe two at the most.

"I would have gone straight through the windshield, as would Craig.

"Suffice it to say that since then, I have always driven that corner carefully."

If you curve around onto North Road, you will have the chance to turn left onto State Road and head past a glass-blowing facility and a pottery studio with a permanent pricey-looking, hand-painted wooden SALE sign in front.

You will also pass Cronig's, a locally owned grocery store with two branches, which pioneered the notion of the "Our Island Card." Full-time residents of the island over the age of eighteen can join for a modest fee and receive discounts everywhere on the island. Cronig's itself has offered as much as 20 percent off.

The town of Tisbury includes the harbor of Vineyard Haven, the site of Carly Simon's Five Corners ("Why, there was a traffic jam, a real traffic jam. In Vineyard Haven! This afternoon!"). As the ferry pulls into Vineyard Haven, you can see the homes of some of the more prominent Vineyarders, including Rose and William Styron's, a house whose porch rivals the one at the Chilmark General Store for spirited conversation and an outdoor shower that attracted a long list of famous guests, among them, Frank Sinatra. In Vineyard Haven you can find bracelets and earrings and pendants shaped like a map of the island, you can find fudge, and you can shop at Midnight Farm: gauze skirts for about $300, expensive bedding, and rustic pre-dented furniture. The Black Dog Tavern, with its line of souvenirs branded by the silhouette of a black Lab, is right next to the staging area for the ferry. Adam Sandler, playing an understanding husband, wears one of its T-shirts in the movie *Spanglish*. They are the clothing of choice in Barcelona or Dublin for students studying abroad. Vineyard Haven is usually quiet at night, but it does jam on occasion, such as when the Bunch of Grapes Bookstore organized midnight celebrations of the release of yet another Harry Potter book and during its annual street fair.

Oak Bluffs (also known as OB): gingerbread architecture, a revivalist campground, and an annual celebration in August known as Illumination Night. Illumination Night sounds like it should be the title of a novel, which in fact it is, by Alice Hoffman. On that evening in August, the gingerbread cottages in the old Methodist prayer camp in Oak Bluffs are draped with lanterns and lit, while songs fill the air from the stage at the tabernacle, songs about grand old flags and paper moons and how this land belongs to you and me.

Every summer morning at around eleven a.m. in Oak Bluffs, the Flying Horses Carousel, the nation's oldest, announces it is open with canned carnival music joining the squeals of children and the molecular odor of each attention-getting kernel of popcorn. Circuit Avenue, the main street, one way, heading inland, takes its travelers past souvenir shops and a hardware store (where, at least in my experience, you can get a mallet for pounding meat but forget about kitchen twine) and restaurants like the Sweet Life Café.

Jill Nelson documented the hold Oak Bluffs has had over the black middle and upper classes in America in her book *Finding Martha's Vineyard: African Americans at Home on an Island*:

> From the 1940s onward the number of African Americans on the Vineyard has increased dramatically. Black vacationers, many of whom became homeowners, began arriving on the Vineyard after World War Two, first renting and later purchasing houses in the Highlands and spreading out to buy houses closer to town and the beach. While African-American homeowners are predominantly in Oak Bluffs, the most integrated of the six towns, in recent decades increasing numbers of African Americans have purchased or built homes all around the island. When it comes to buying property on the Vineyard these days, class, and the financial ability it brings with it, for the most part trumps race.

When Barack Obama and his family came to the island for their first visit during his presidency in 2009, DeNeen Brown of the *Washington Post* wrote a piece headlined: "Oak Bluffs, Mass., Is Where the Black Elite Is at Home in the Summer."

"Oak Bluffs," wrote Brown, "once a Methodist summer retreat where anti-racism sermons were preached, has drawn blacks since the 1800s. Some came as servants to wealthy white families. Others worked in the hotels. Eventually, elite blacks from New York, Boston, and Washington retreated here for summer vacations, many buying houses in an area they called the Oval or the Highlands, which Harlem Renaissance writer Dorothy West wrote about toward the end of her career in her 1995 novel, *The Wedding*."

Brown quotes West: "They formed a fortress, a bulwark of colored society. Their occupants could boast that they, or even better their ancestors, had owned a home away from home since the days when a summer hegira was taken by few colored people above the rank of servant."

Brown's article provided a roll call of prominent black visitors to the island, past and present: singer Paul Robeson, composer Harry T. Burleigh, Massachusetts senator Edward Brooke, Martin Luther King Jr., Spike Lee, former adviser to President Clinton Vernon Jordan, and Obama adviser Valerie Jarrett.

Edgartown: a whaling port now transformed into a tasseled loafer of a place, with narrow sidewalks and clam-shelled driveways. The men wear brick-red Bermuda shorts secured by belts with anchor themes, and women can choose between expensive silk or madras hairbands, at stores whose names are cute beyond measure, like Whistling Fish. The BE BACK IN A MINUTE signs tend to be hand-painted with floral borders: Edgartown does not encourage provisional solutions such as Post-it notes. The street North Spyglass Lane is begging to be the name of a children's picture book.

Like all islands, the Vineyard is a head case, mysterious, a unique coinage, cut off, stuck-up, a loner, a bit of a drama queen. Newcomers sometimes experience the island as snobby, and not just in the obvious terms of how much property you own and its value. The island sometimes feels like a club with secret rules that no one appears all that eager to share. It can take years of island living to learn beyond which desultory dirt road lurks the world-class beach or to know who to call when the well goes dry and where to go to get the best bass bait. The island is filled with hierarchies, an obvious one being the length of time you, and ideally your ancestors, have been coming to or living there. Purple is the Vineyard neutral. You have cachet if your phone number begins with the old 693 exchange and if you know that Lucy Vincent Beach was also known as Jungle Beach and before that as the Blue Mailbox Beach as well as the nude beach. Posters from the Hot Tin Roof, a nightspot that opened at the airport in 1979, are envied in direct proportion to how long ago the event being promoted was held. Even better if you can claim to have heard James Taylor perform as a fifteen-year-old at the Moon-Cusser coffeehouse in Oak Bluffs, when the *Gazette* proclaimed him "probably the most outstanding young folksinger on the Island." A T-shirt with a big *A* and an asterisk shows that you frequented Aboveground Records before it closed in 2013. Prepare to wait in line at Ice House Pond if you want to swim: only four cars are allowed in the parking lot at any time, and in order to protect the clear water from contamination, boogie boards and flotation devices are forbidden, though I have a friend who somehow gets away with goggles and a snorkel.

Lamentation for defunct restaurants and businesses is another way to demonstrate a social edge. Remember Feasts in Chilmark? Take It Easy Baby in Oak Bluffs? The Wesley Hotel in Oak Bluffs before it got a chic makeover and changed its name to Summercamp? Bramhall & Dunn, a curated emporium of kilim rugs, quilts, sweaters, handbags, and tableware, on Main Street in Vineyard Haven that closed in 2011? Smoke 'N Bones?

The more you can fold in the names of old-timers, deceased or otherwise, into conversation and make it seem as if you knew them personally, the better—George Manter, Henry Beetle Hough, Bea Whiting, Donald DeSorcy, anyone with the last name of Vanderhoop or Mayhew or Pease or Norton or Daggett or Flanders, to name just a few.

If you are someone who remembers, and can therefore tease, the winners of the prizes at a costume party at the Agricultural Hall on October 27, 1947 ("most horrible" to John Alley, George Churchill, and Judith Cronig; "most attractive" to Karen Barker as Little Red Riding Hood, Carol Spencer as Cinderella, and Margaret Duquette as a little old-fashioned lady), you occupy an aristocracy that has a strong element of New England one-upmanship: roots and respect are often intertwined. The rest of us have to rely on the town columns in the *Gazette* for this sort of insider information.

The terms "up-island" and "down-island" are a source of confusion. It is easy to assume they refer to north and south. In fact, the western part of the island is called up-island and the eastern part is called down-island. The expression comes from the direction of boats crossing from New England to England, with England being ground zero, and therefore "down" as you sail closer to it and "up" as you sail away from it.

Martha's Vineyard likes its fences, especially in the form of old stone walls. It also likes its annual rituals and prizes the slow rhythm of a place that lives off land and sea. The Martha's Vineyard Agricultural Society Fair in August is run by a group of women who meet all year and really care about who grows the juiciest tomato or the largest cabbage in both the junior and the adult division and who stitches the finest quilt in seventeen different categories and who shucks clams the fastest. A skillet throw (the missile is custom-made of steel and weighs approximately three pounds and eleven ounces) is open to "women the world over," as if females flinging frying pans is a certifiably global impulse. Cattle and goats and lambs and ducks and cocks and hens and hares and rabbits and pigeons enter endless competitions. Dogs who win best in show get their pictures in the paper: Ridge and Elvis and Sheba and Winslow and Lucy and all those Luckys who really are lucky. Rivalry is everywhere, among flowers and pickles and cupcakes, as well as for the "Best Display of American Pride." The draft horse pulling competition is a signature event. One old-timer told the *Gazette* that the horses, which weigh more than 1,600 pounds, are capable of "pulling all day if you let them. Those are the horses that built a nation." The fair is a peaceable kingdom, its own mini-world of manure and flies that need swatting, of cotton candy and corn dogs.

Summer visitors, lunging after the feeling of well-being that vacation is supposed to provide, often experience the island in a state of willful amnesia. This impulse to gloss over unpleasantness of any kind takes the form of seeking out and celebrating Faux Woes, also known as Designer Anguish.

One summer the papers were filled with news of litigation between the Black Dog people and some upstarts who were marketing a knockoff T-shirt featuring a far less upbeat motif: Dead Dog.

The most enduring of Faux Woes may well be the Pie Wars, a controversy of many years' duration, with various claimants—some now out of business—having arisen as to who is best: Eileen Blake? The Scottish Bakehouse? The Black Dog? Morning Glory Farm? Humphreys? The Pie Chicks?

Also, disagreements as to styles and flavors:

Lattice-topped? Double-crusted?

Apple? Apple crumb? Blueberry? Strawberry-rhubarb? Peach? Pumpkin?

Anne once gave this shopping pointer:

Go to the West Tisbury Farmers Mkt.
Go directly to stand of Ms. Judie Gersh
Purchase pie or pies (one for your own self)
I know they're expensive, but mmmm good! Okay, now you can
*   buy vegetables and flowers*
Pug proverb: one blueberry-peach pie is equal to 1,000,000,000
*   cups of kibble*

A friend named Sue Banta who usually visits the island for a month with her husband and four children and their frequent guests showed me sixty empty pie cartons in her recycle bin and that was only halfway through her vacation. When our favorite pie source, the Island Bake Shop, also known as Humphreys on State Road in West Tisbury, moved elsewhere, we suffered the disruption as a personal loss. Sawhorses and cinder block obstacles blocked the entrance at its old location in West Tisbury. White on the inside, the shop was tucked into a pristine wooded setting with a picnic table set amid lots of shade. Catering to sugar pilgrims, it had the calming air of a sanitarium. Its only flaw was the famously inconvenient telephone pole in front. One time, we saw a customer backing out too quickly, smashing his taillight and shattering the back window, thus purchasing what was possibly the world's most expensive doughnut. Now a big new house occupies the spot. The telephone pole has not budged.

The Cadillac of Faux Woes involved the *Queen Elizabeth 2*, which was supposed to dock on the island one summer's day. The *Gazette* reported that for its transatlantic voyage, the vessel stocked up on "30,000 eggs, 500 cans of tinned fruit, and 50 pounds of dog biscuits. She carries four professional printers on her staff, six dancers, but oddly enough, only one radio officer and one bellboy. She needs 531 tons of water simply to do her guests' laundry for five days. She needs 4,000 cigars to keep her men happy."

Before its fateful non-arrival, the local media glowed with welcome, as if each of the one-thousand-plus passengers was a dignitary, when in fact the true dignitaries were, obviously, their pocketbooks. Owners of boutiques and restaurants posted welcome signs, but it was not to be. The boat grounded several miles off-island, sustaining a seventy-four-foot gash on its starboard side. Since it had run aground, it was never in danger of sinking. The *Gazette* was the only paper to get a reporter on board and was so proud to have a scoop that someone said it should win the award for Public Service Breathlessness.

One year the Faux Woe was entirely intellectual in nature, existing mostly in the letters to the editor. A reader wrote: "We were driving by Beetlebung Corner the other day and noticed *it* was missing." The letter inspired a summer-long rebuttal in the pages of the paper about what "it" might be and whether "it" had ever been there in the first place. Connoisseurs of such matters remember the correspondence as folderol of an especially high grade of inutility, worthy of the *Times* of London.

In 1984, Lillian Hellman, famous Vineyard summer person, had the bad timing to die around the same time as a year-rounder much beloved in the community and contributor to island life in dozens of ways.

Hellman wrote plays, memoirs, and essays in a career that began in the 1930s with her first play, *The Children's Hour*, in which a young girl accuses two female teachers of what amounted to misconduct at the time. Hellman often said that the play is "not about lesbianism. It's about the power of a lie." When she was summoned to appear before the House Un-American Activities Committee, she refused to testify: "To hurt innocent people whom I knew many years ago in order to save myself is, to me, inhuman and indecent and dishonorable. I cannot and will not cut my conscience to fit this year's fashions, even though I long ago came to the conclusion that I was not a political person and could have no comfortable place in any political group." In 1973, she published *Pentimento*, a reminiscence about a friendship with a woman named Julia who was trapped inside Nazi Germany. In her introduction to the book, Hellman explained the title this way:

Old paint on canvas, as it ages, sometimes becomes transparent. When that happens it is possible, in some pictures, to see the original lines: a tree will show through a

woman's dress, a child makes way for a dog, a large boat
is no longer on an open sea. That is called pentimento
because the painter "repented," changed his mind.

The veracity of her memoir was called into question, eventually leading the acid-tongued Mary McCarthy to declare to talk
show host Dick Cavett: "Everything she writes is a lie, including
'and' and 'the.'" Hellman slapped her rival with a $2.5 million
lawsuit, causing McCarthy to further bait Hellman: "If someone
had told me, 'Don't say anything about Lillian Hellman because
she'll sue you,' it wouldn't have stopped me. It might have spurred
me on." The suit was dropped when Hellman died.

As I remember it, in some views the *Gazette* gave too much
play to Hellman and not enough to the year-rounder, thus angering
the natives who could not understand how a mere summertime
scamp could command so much ink, which in turn riled the mere
summertime scamps who could not understand the provincialism
that would equate a mere year-rounder with a Person of Literary
Stature.

In general the obituaries in the *Gazette* for older island residents, full-time and part-time, are often a treat (unless . . .).

One recent notice recalled that the deceased met his future
wife, "a city girl from Lowell," while she taught business education
in Oak Bluffs. Their first date? Shooting rats at the town dump. (Be
kind: this couple had gone through the Depression and the war and
they were now footloose at last, but likely on a limited budget. In
any event, the real story is why this wasn't their last date.)

When an astrologer, whose real name was Barbara but who
also went by "Nighthorse," died, her family asked that in lieu of

flowers people "work to heal the planet environmentally and politically." A businessman's widow and children suggested that people honor him by staking the person behind them at Espresso Love or Dippin Donuts to a free cup of coffee. Someone else would like to be remembered by a brick at the bandstand in Oak Bluffs, a bench or lantern. A sports fisherman requested that his surf-casting pals at Nomans release a fish back into the sea. Someone else wants his ashes "scattered to the seven seas and four winds" and he would like his mourners to "give a flower to a loved one or friend; call that relative, friend, or classmate you haven't spoken to in way too long."

Obituaries often include a person's long-ago summer employment.

The family of woodworker Noah Block wanted the world to know that as a teenager he "hayed for Leonard Athearn in Chilmark; worked at Farmer Greene's in North Tisbury; delivered garments for Oak Bluffs dry cleaner Harold Butler, and, most happily, learned something of the building trade from Roger Allen of Chilmark, and baked brownies at Argie and Bernice Humphrey's North Tisbury Bakery." Mary Fischer's obit noted that she delivered milk for "old Fred Fisher at Nip 'n' Tuck Farm . . . sold tickets for the Steamship Authority, working with old Howie Leonard in the Oak Bluffs terminal . . . and cooked for Haynes Restaurant (now State Road)."

By Vineyard standards, these are robust and admirable résumés.

Even pre-obituary, memories of having held certain summer jobs are a badge on the island, whether the work was backbreaking (picking any of the ten different kinds of lettuce at Morning Glory Farm, especially if you biked there in the predawn hours) or cool (bartending at the Kelley House pub) or high-toned (being a hostess at Atria in Edgartown) or classic (scooping ice cream at Mad Martha's) or mundane (freezing in the excessive summertime AC while you bagged groceries at Stop & Shop).

Jen Tyson, a frequent visitor from Amherst who stayed with Claire and Hilary Lawlor, based her college essay on her mundane and not-so-mundane experience at Stop & Shop one summer while living with Claire in Oak Bluffs:

Once on the Woods Hole–Vineyard Haven ferry, with the sun reflecting over the ocean, I felt truly euphoric. The sensation of nirvana was short-lived, only to be replaced by anxiety about the prospect of finding a summer job. My plan for the "perfect summer" hinged upon becoming gainfully employed. After being on-island for a week and having applied to Mad Martha's, the best ice cream place on-island; David Ryan's, an upscale restaurant in Edgartown; and all the other equally appealing places, I had no job offers. With the very real possibility of being ejected from my ideal living situation (my best friend's parents' house without her parents), I decided to swallow my pride and apply to Stop & Shop. It turned out that I was regarded as something of a hot commodity there. Once they learned that I had my own car, housing on-island, no other job and no children in tow, they hired me on the spot.

My first eight-hour shift was quite an experience. I was asked to put groceries in plastic, then in paper, and finally in plastic again. I was to bag the English cucumbers separately from the pickling cucumbers. I was expected to comply, apologize, smile, and pretend that the self-serving requests and demands of the vacationers were completely acceptable while they looked at me as if I were a lackadaisical moron. However, the greatest challenge to my self-image was the grotesque, polyester, collared, green Stop & Shop shirt ornamented with a name tag upon which my name had been scrawled, seemingly by somebody's left foot. The only size available was XL, the material gave me a rash, and I was not comfortable with the stigma that was attached to wearing that shirt. I thought I would immediately be categorized by customers with people like the baggers at my local Stop & Shop, one of whom recites Oscar winners from the last thirty years over and over while he works. I also despised the notion that strangers would not only be able to boss me around and belittle me, but that they would also be able to personalize the experience by using my name.

After my first forty-hour week, I became rather disenchanted with the job. My friend had landed a position as hostess at an elegant and very expensive restaurant. Her job was to look pretty and greet people while shaking their hands and on occasion getting palmed twenty-dollar bills. She never missed an opportunity to make fun of me for my job, thus affirming and promoting my snobbish tendencies. Because I was surrounded by the excess that dominated Martha's Vineyard, it was hard to face the realization that I didn't belong on a yacht or driving a Mercedes, but rather behind the cash register and driving my uncle's '91 Geo Metro.

As the days progressed, I began to get to know my co-workers. I learned that most of them lived on-island year-round, and Stop & Shop was their reality. Some were single parents, some were people my grandparents' age who had been working there for over twenty years, and others were fourteen-year-olds forced to work in order to supplement their family's income. I was the exception; nobody else I worked with was in the same position as me. I was seventeen with no comparable responsibilities. I was barely different from the entitled vacationers who made my job so lamentable. Before last summer, most of the adults whom I had been intimately acquainted with had PhDs, MDs, or their own studios. I was unprepared to befriend individuals who were forty years my senior with an equivalent of an eighth grade education. These people have been working the same job for years. I felt it unfair that my biggest concern was, When can I go to the beach? Or should I call back that cute guy from behind the counter at the Black Dog Bakery? I didn't think my co-workers and I would ever be able to relate, because if I was in their position I would resent the overprivileged teenager who felt that the 10:00 a.m. shift was too early and who spent the less busy times sending and receiving text messages on her cell phone. However, to my surprise I was accepted into the Vineyard Haven Stop & Shop family with open arms. My co-workers didn't seem to mind that I rarely donned the green shirt or that I constantly drank smoothies on the job. Whenever I would get a big order I could count on Barbara to help me bag. When lecherous old men tried to persuade me to "get a bite to eat after my shift," I knew Tim would put a brotherly arm around my shoulder and offer to take the offending customer "outside for a chat." I assume my co-workers hated their job even more than I did, but they all wore that awful shirt coupled with a smile every day.

I never saw Tom Hanks or any other celebrities rumored to be on the island. However, I did meet Jarret, a nineteen-year-old from the mainland who drove two hours from the mainland to the ferry every morning and two hours home from the ferry every night, seven days a week, to support his girlfriend and her children. I also met Lajah, who came to Martha's Vineyard to escape a life of inner-city crime and drug abuse. During my interactions with other employees, I began to value the education I have been fortunate enough to receive and the future opportunities I will have which far surpass receiving the long-sleeve manager's version of a hideous green shirt that signifies promotion at Stop & Shop.

I grew not only to embrace but to cherish the bubble of relative poverty I had stumbled upon that set me apart from the Lilly Pulitzer–garbed, self-proclaimed Vineyarders. Now as I sit at home, finding the limit as x approaches infinity or trying to formulate a thesis connecting cross-dressing Shakespearean women to societal gender roles, I no longer resent losing sleep or missing the concerts all my friends are going to. I consider myself lucky to have the opportunity to stress out over grades, exams, and, most recently, college application essays such as this one.

Chapter Four

The New House

The living room in the house that Donald DeSorcy built for the Katzenbachs in 1978 combined the old and the new. It had sliding glass doors for walls, modern and daring, but it also had a mantel and two buttresses bolted into the ceiling that DeSorcy repurposed from driftwood rescued from a boat shipwrecked in the 1800s. Soon enough, the house began to show its age, caught in the slow progression in which patina eventually routs novelty. Tables tilted, beds sagged, screens rusted, doors warped. Shell ashtrays remained unmoved for years with the same pennies and ponytail holders and paper clips, curled up, catatonic, nestled in their scalloped insides.

A separate wing emanated off the living room, with two small bedrooms and a bathroom with a blue-tiled shower in between them. You had to walk outside to get to those rooms and also to the self-standing master bedroom, whose shower boasted red-hot tile. The master bedroom, with windows on all sides, had the feel of a boat. The weather floated in and out, like snippets of an overheard conversation: fog, wind, and sunlight. In the 1980s, with the arrival of six grandchildren, two small bedrooms and an outdoor shower were added off the kitchen.

The idea of outbuildings was a modification of a design common in the Adirondacks, where Lydia spent her childhood summers on Pearl Island.

Across the pond, a red barn with the clean lines of a certain kind of realistic painting inspired many sketches as well as meditations.

A college boy once wrote in the logs:

As I sit here in wonder, thinking about the red barn across the pond, then thinking, Why am I thinking about a silly red barn? *it hits me smack in the face.* It is precisely because I can sit here and think about silly red barns while my nose peels from the sun. While we're at it, who is Martha anyway?

(As you might suspect, he was a philosophy major.)

Decking united all the rooms and created a traffic pattern that funneled everyone outside as much as possible.

The colors of the interior were subdued, so as not to compete with the outdoors.

A few items survived the long-ago sale of John's mother's Pearl Island house, including two torture-quality stiff brown wicker chairs at least one hundred years old. They had a penance-exacting air of disapproval, like the sour expressions of chaperones at dances for young people. Lydia exhibited boundless loyalty to these chairs, and if you were foolish enough to advance the notion that they might be profitably replaced by something more comfortable, something upholstered, something that felt less explicitly like a pincushion, you earned a blank imperious stare.

Also from Pearl Island, a small dark wooden table with loose slats and wobbly legs that had once served as a surface for servants when they ironed and a tall green bureau that stored string, ribbons, candles, lotions, nail clippers, crayons, scissors, Band-Aids, sparklers, tape measures, and matches.

The simplicity of the furnishings and their well-worn familiarity were what accounted for their value.

On the shore facing south huge boulders had been trucked in as a bulwark against erosion. The ocean is not easily bullied; the rocks would pack the might of feathers if a real hurricane ever made a direct hit.

John and I decided to get married in May 1980 in Eugene O'Neill territory in Connecticut, where most of my family lived. We found a tiny Catholic church without heat, used only in the summer for seasonal visitors, and we found a priest who gave us the impression that he was about to leave the day after our wedding for an out-of-state treatment center in order to dry out. Lydia had offered to raid her apparently endless trove of prestigious Episcopalian bishops, but I was clear that I wanted my heritage on full display. To me the Episcopalian religion was Catholicism without the dread: What good was that? After the ceremony we walked from Saint Joseph's downhill a few hundred feet to the Ram Island Yacht Club, low-key and weatherworn, secured by a friend of the family's. The band was a bunch of schoolteachers my sisters taught with. I think the food was chicken à la king; I know it was forgettable. My favorite comment about the wedding came from my uncle, Dermot:

"I've not seen a wedding like this since the war—so many people from out of town. No, nothing like it since the war."

I was pregnant before a year of marriage was up.

By early 1981, John and I found ourselves at a medical office in South Miami examining a grainy piece of paper that looked like a satellite shot. The technology of sonograms was in its own infancy. We gazed at what looked like a lot of dark blobs, but according to the technician, if you held it up to the light and squinted just so, it could be argued, given how the shadows fell, that our boy might be a boy.

The labor was a nightmare of extra innings, taking twenty-seven hours, and when our son arrived, thanks to an emergency C-section at the wholly inconvenient time of 3:41 a.m. on August 21, 1981, we joked that he came into this world already showing a will of his own. I was among the first in our group of friends to have a child. Like us, they were in the business of gathering news. Being persistent by virtue of their profession, they kept calling the hospital to determine my progress, identifying themselves by their places of employment, saying they were from the *Miami Herald*, and the *Miami News*, and the Associated Press, and ABC News, and the *Washington Post*, and even the old *Washington Star*. The credentials and the urgency of my friends misled the public relations department at South Miami Hospital into thinking it had a celebrity birth on its hands. After discovering that was not the case, one of the hospital bureaucrats looked at me, sadly, and said, "If only you had been Cher. Or someone."

Our daughter arrived in January 1986 in Cambridge, Massachusetts, where I had a fellowship. This time the birth was all in day's work, starting at eight a.m. and over by eight at night.

All during the labor I dreamed of one perfectly cooked egg. After delivery, Justine was quiet and alert, appearing to be already taking notes. One of Nick's gifts to me as a son was to make me feel that I had learned something the first time around. Everything was easier with Justine because her brother had led the way.

One of my many mantras is that in life we either repeat or we repair, and I wanted to give my children more attention, more bounty, more pleasure than I remember from my all-bets-are-off childhood. And what better place than in a perfectly secluded spot on Martha's Vineyard two weeks every year when everyone's only job was to have a good time?

As the family grew, our simple baggage became more complicated. Backpacks got replaced by mortgages and Datsun 240Zs by Volvo station wagons with roof racks. Self-centered quiet gave way to the clamor of children, and life morphed into a series of quarterly tax payments and car pools to soccer fields. The denser our lives got, the more crucial it was to stay true to Thumb Point. For John and me our visits to the island were a kind of theme song, a dependable riff in lives that, like all lives, sometimes lost their harmony.

We repeat or we repair: I am sure the logs were about both impulses. Despite all the pressures on her, my mother kept scrapbooks of our schoolwork and our drawings and even letters to famous people that obviously never got sent, such as the letters to Dear Abby and to the president of the John Birch Society. I wanted to create a similar legacy.

The Katzenbachs vacationed in a sequence, dividing the summer months into two-week parcels in a kind of tag-team approach. We sometimes overlapped by design, but only for a day or two. Anne and Steve liked the island when it was quiet and so chose June and mid- to late September whenever possible. We liked the first two weeks in August. Christopher favored June and July. Mimi picked various times, her schedule tied in part to when her son, Avery, would also be visiting his dad's family house up-island on Menemsha Pond.

Trying to figure out who in the family got to be there when was never easy, made worse by some people's willingness (ours) to commit in January to an allotted time and others who preferred last-minute arrangements. We heard of families who had managed to come up with a document spelling out how time got divided to the minute, but the Katzenbachs' efforts in this direction always fizzled out. John and his siblings are so distinct from one another in personality, so certain of how they personally wish to navigate the planet, so opinionated (having a lawyer for a father and a psycho-analyst for a mother probably helped in this regard), that they did not mesh together the way siblings sometimes do, with that kind of mushy interchangeability that can be charming or off-putting, depending. It hit me at some point along the way that they were all so independent and outspoken and confident, it was as if each had been an only child.

Even in the new house, John's parents tried to cling to as many of their old ways as long as possible. For a long time the generations divided. John's parents held the torch for ruggedness and we, especially when our children were young, begged for modern conveniences. Back in the days of diapers, we spent a lot of vacation time at the Airport Laundromat.

The new house had no electricity and the daily lighting of the kerosene lamps was an exercise in patience and exactitude, guided by John's father's written instructions:

The key to having no problems is to scrape the wick every time you fill them. To scrape: remove round metal piece in middle of wick. Insert scraper (gray plastic wheel) and turn several times. Maintain tension on knob that raises wick so that it really scrapes the carbon off. Buy only best quality kerosene. Start slowly: mantle barely glowing. Spare mantles in the bookcase; spare wicks, chimneys in storeroom. Never leave lamps burning when you are away from the house.

Artifacts from the shack made a sentimental transition to the new dwelling, including a gas-powered refrigerator. We called it "placebo icebox," because although it looked the part of a modern metallic contrivance dedicated to cold storage, it never in fact cooled anything. A guest who praised the glory of the ocean and the Big Dipper so thoughtfully placed outside her bedroom window also noted, "On a more banal level, the icebox is dying; it should be put out of its misery; replace it before it sours more milk!"

In time, the kerosene lamps were replaced with electricity, and a private generator supplied hot water. Eventually, a washer and dryer took up a corner in the kitchen next to the new fridge.

Most miraculous of all: one summer in the mid-1980s we arrived on the island to find that a phone line had been installed under the pond, the handiwork of our cryptic neighbor who kept making appearances in the log.

Dirt road now a superhighway: Mal had a busy winter.

Mal replaced phone line. Oysters on old line. Listening in?

Mal, Mal, Mal: here, there, and everywhere. Was he even real?

For many years I thought Mal Jones did not in fact exist, that he was a folk legend, a pond-side sprite or a rogue angel. But if he didn't exist, how else could we explain the series of marvels that kept getting attributed to him for which he appeared to demand no payment and even less applause?

One time some neighbors complained that too many cars passed in front of their property. So in the winter when everyone else was back in the city—heeding the calls of the megaphone men, the hucksters and money guys; inventing new slogans for old products; jockeying for an even better cubicle; slaving over an elaborate brief—Mal Jones allegedly took his earth mover and made a new road.

And then, when we wanted a phone line, he found some cable and installed it in the ponds, which worked, for a while.

He apparently could read nature perfectly. He decoded the pond so when it was time to open the cut and replenish it with ocean water, he was always among the first to know. The water level of the pond would be high, the moon full.

The town uses large machines to create the cut. In the old days, a wooden dredge, drawn by either horse or oxen, with a human guide, did the work. The channel is dug across the barrier beach that then allows salt water to enter the pond with the purpose of stimulating shellfish growth. It begins as a narrow tunnel, expanding so that it is a huge muddy torrent that tames itself in a few days' time. Especially frightening in the early stages, the cut lasts two or three weeks. Riding its current, often with wet suits and boogie boards, whether the tide is going in or out, is a daylong activity.

If you brought Mal Jones a homemade pie by way of thanking him for a favor, as my neighbor Danica Kombol once did, he was likely to return the gesture by offering you a frozen container of his famous raccoon stew.

When, in the early 1990s, the pump wheezed its last wheeze and went kaput at the measly level of twenty pounds of pressure, Anne wrote a poem by way of tribute:

> *The era of the new pump dawns*
> *And I'm at a loss for words*
> *How can this be Thumb Point*
> *If disaster never occurs?*

> *The logs will go untouched*
> *Now we have electrical power*
> *No time for me to write*
> *Because I'm taking a shower*

> *A day at the beach is nice*
> *But nothing matches the pleasure*
> *Of waking up in the morning*
> *To unlimited water pressure*

We once had a competition to name the most controversial addition to the household decor, a piece of driftwood—a conglomeration of roots that jutted wildly, with a span of at least four feet. Rescued from the shoreline by Donald DeSorcy, it hung on a thick rusting chain from the ceiling in the middle of the living room.

Over the years, we called it the Alien, the Hanging Unit, and Animal Number 12, after the urban myth term for an animal with no head, just a ton of extra breasts and legs, the mutant source of chicken nuggets used in fast-food restaurants. Someone said it looked like Meryl Streep swooping across the screen in *Angels in America*. Someone else: a paddle fan on an acid trip. John's father suggested naming it De Sorcerer, after Donald.

The Hanging Unit had a suitor. It inspired this ode by a visitor, a poet named Peter Richards, who had been dating one of our babysitters:

> *Some of your guests enjoy this antler alternative*
> *Hung high above where roots are accustomed to be.*
> *Dry, sprawling, and floating forever—*
> *A chandelier the heavens can see.*
> *Roofs whisper to windows that listen.*

Lydia loved its amorphous mysteries. Were the branches writhing or dancing? Did they sob or grin? I viewed it less fondly as something you might see in the kind of tavern where the proprietor thinks it is appealing to have nets with rubber lobsters in them and to leave Christmas decorations up all year round. In order to get rid of it, we tried to appeal to Lydia's desire to be original, telling her we saw versions *exactly like it* at Home Depot under the brand name Driftolier, but she saw right through that. She knew unique when she saw it.

One of my favorite memories of the island was seeing my father-in-law, Nick, pulling into the dirt driveway after a long drive from Princeton, New Jersey, the town where he was born, where he went to college, and where he spent a good portion of his adult life. Often described by the press as a bear of man—tall, big-boned, deep-voiced—in age he lost some height. His natural athletic gifts had eroded as well due to a crippling condition called Paget's disease: not a picnic, a defect in the process of bone growth causing affected areas to bow out and become soft, a condition likely exacerbated by the malnutrition he experienced in a POW camp. Shortly after arrival, car unloaded, dogs fed and watered, he appeared, for a moment, incorporeal, floating, free at last of gravity and pain as he eased his increasingly recalcitrant bones into one of the chairs on the deck late in the day, just before dinner, a glass containing liquid often of a martini nature in hand, dogs at his side. He would then stare at the expanse that unfolded in front of him.

"There may be other places in the world that are as beautiful," he often said in his careful, lawyerly way, mindful that distinctions matter, "but I doubt there are any that are more beautiful."

When he could still move about a bit, he loved using the Sailfish, but those days ended in the early 1980s. The only time I ever saw him in the motorboat was when my son was five and Nick allowed him to drive his grandfather around the pond in the rain. It must have been physically harrowing for him, but he did it anyway.

While on the island, John's father liked to assign himself a task purely physical in nature that he proceeded to perform with grace and cheer. His approach to ceiling repair, the green garbage bag route, has already been documented. He was the king of errands: if someone needed a stick of butter, he would drive to Alley's to get it. John's father was familiar with the drill at Machine and Marine in Vineyard Haven: he would drop off his outboard engine that needed fixing along with everyone else's engines that needed fixing, and then wait forever. It was his job to de-tick the dogs. He also de-skunked them on occasion. As he roamed the property, he exhibited the same puttering benevolence and goofy peace of Marlon Brando at the end of *The Godfather*. You had to wonder what was on the mind of this dignified man, used to arguing abstruse matters in court. Perhaps on the island he was reassured by the concreteness of the tasks that anchored his day, relieved to be trimming poison ivy rather than tweaking the fine print in a codicil, swinging on birches instead of studying Latin.

Accolades and biographical details trailed him: his father had been attorney general for the state of New Jersey, his mother was a well-known educator who founded what eventually became known as the Marie H. Katzenbach School for the Deaf; he played hockey at Exeter, he traveled in Europe by bike in the summer of 1939 with some high school buddies, he went to Princeton, he left school in 1942 to join the service. His plane was shot down in Sicily. When the navigator announced that the engine was on fire, Nick, a master of understatement, knowing they had less than thirty seconds to touch down, said, "That's too bad." He spent almost three years as a prisoner of war in German-occupied Poland. The Red Cross was allowed to provide food and books. Whenever a cake appeared, the person who cut it got the last piece to ensure precise portions, a relief from the usual menu—wormy bread, thin soup, rotten rutabagas. He finished college when he got back to the States in 1945, taking exams based on the books he studied at the camp. He met Lydia at a wedding in Washington, D.C. Like so many young men returning from the war, he could not wait to taste a crisp apple and to feel the lips of a woman against his own.

They married in June 1946, a year that had the largest marriage rate per capita in the United States up to that point: if you got hitched, you were a demographic cliché.

For once in her life, Lydia was thrilled to be trite.

Then law school at Yale, a Rhodes Scholarship to England, a professorship at the University of Chicago, a Ford Foundation grant for a year in Switzerland, a call from the White House to join the best and the brightest, a move to Highland Place and the District of Columbia. Four children born between 1949 and 1959.

From their young years as a married couple, this story, a family staple:

While at Oxford, very early in their time together, living in a Quonset hut, Lydia decided she needed to demonstrate all the necessary wifely skills (beyond getting pregnant), so while her husband was in class, she spent the day preparing a most special dinner, aware that only a few years earlier he had been starving.

Roast beef with all the sides.

Vanilla ice cream with chocolate sauce for dessert.

She slaved all day in the barely functioning kitchen, and when he came through the door, the feast was on the table. She had made one small miscalculation. She had placed the chocolate sauce for dessert in a small container that looked eerily like a . . . gravy bowl. Before she could stop him, he had poured chocolate sauce all over the roast beef and the mashed potatoes.

Lydia was about to dissolve into tears of failure.

Nick, recognizing his mistake, said nothing.

He tucked in his napkin, lifted his fork, and proceeded to eat the entire plate of food.

And then, at the end, he said it was the best meal he had ever had.

As deputy attorney general under Robert Kennedy, Nick was sent to the University of Mississippi to escort James Meredith to class and to the University of Alabama, where he stood in the schoolhouse door staring down Governor George Wallace who was intent on preventing Vivian Malone and James Hood from attending classes. You can see him in film footage from that era, telling Wallace the time had come to integrate the University of Alabama—a moment that lives on as a cultural wink in the movie *Forrest Gump*. He used to joke that he was the only one in the family to make it to the big screen.

Under Lyndon Johnson, he was the principal writer of the Voting Rights Act. And when the law passed, he used his high office to ensure that it was enforced, sending examiners to the South to protect black citizens registering to vote.

Vietnam created moral quagmires like a kind of kudzu. No one was immune. Called upon as attorney general to render an opinion as to whether the Gulf of Tonkin Resolution was a legal declaration of war, he said it was. On August 25, 1967, a group of prominent islanders took out an ad condemning his judgment in the *Gazette*.

Early on, I recognized the subject of this ad was best avoided.

The signers were all people of consequence, and as far as I know, Nick and Lydia never socialized with any of them again.

"THE GUT ISSUE"

*"Thereupon Mr. Katzenbach said that
as interesting as the constitutional issue
was, the 'gut issue here is whether or not
the Congress supports the President in
what he does . . .'" New York TIMES,
Aug. 22, 1967.*

Dear Mr. Katzenbach:

We, a group of your summer neighbors on Martha's Vineyard,
wish to express our shock at your recent testimony before the Senate
Foreign Relations Committee and our outrage at your presumption that
Congress, when it passed the Gulf of Tonkin Resolution in 1964, intended to authorize the series of open-ended escalations that now bring
our troop strength in Vietnam up to a half million men and our bomb-
ers within ten miles of the border of China.

We consider your testimony to be the most dangerous sort of
legalistic subterfuge. It may easily be used to prepare Congress and
the American people for the acceptance of any and all further escalations, including war with China, on the basis of a congressional man-
date which, however skillfully argued, cannot be twisted to sanction
World War Three.

"The gut issue" as far as we're concerned is not only whether
"Congress supports what the President does," but whether you, who
we have come to think of as a civilized and humane man, support what
the President does. We urge you as an influential member of
the Administration to stop playing the functionary and speak out
against President Johnson's indefensible diplomacy of violence.

Aaron Asher	*Daniel Lang*
Robert Brustein	*Albert R. Leventhal*
Stanley Burnshaw	*John Marquand*
Jules Feiffer	*Jerry Mason*
Robert Heilbroner	*Philip Rahv*
Lillian Hellman	*Philip Roth*
John Hersey	*Henry Clay Smith*
Henry Beetle Hough	*William Styron*

Kingman Brewster, former president of Yale, defended Nick. From a book titled *The Guardians: Kingman Brewster, His Circle, and the Rise of the Liberal Establishment* by Geoffrey Kabaservice:

> Debates over the war, whether in faculty gatherings or around the dinner table, became sharper, and took a toll on personal relations . . . Brewster wrote a critical letter to the literati. He did not defend his friend Katzenbach's position, but called the ad "bad manners at best" and "an offensive infringement of the long standing ethic of the Vineyard as a place where even a public man's life can be quietly lived." That summer, Brewster and Mac Bundy criticized Brustein over cocktails for breaching long-held (though unwritten) gentlemanly rules of etiquette. Brustein retorted that to keep silent in the face of the war was tantamount to being a "good German."

Lydia had a special place in her heart for Art Buchwald, the rumpled-faced humorist who became island royalty in his later years as he presided as the lead auctioneer at the annual Possible Dreams Auction, always capping off the evening literally by doffing his cap and taking bids on it.

He wrote this column shortly after the ad appeared:

> Although we've had a certain amount of inclement weather up here, Martha's Vineyard has had a long hot summer. In previous years the great issues at stake on this tiny island

off the coast of Cape Cod have had to do with zoning laws, protection of wildlife in the ponds and debates on ways of saving the sandy cliffs at Gay Head.

But this year the Vietnam war has raised its ugly head. The big "gut" issue on Martha's Vineyard is: Do you or do you not spoil the vacation of the United States undersecretary of state who happens to vacation up here in the summertime?

What happened was that Undersecretary of State Nicholas Katzenbach testified a few weeks ago before the Senate Foreign Relations Committee in Washington on the legal aspects of the 1964 Gulf of Tonkin resolution. As might be expected, he defended President Johnson's policies. This incensed a group of Martha's Vineyard summer people and they decided to take a full page advertisement in the *Vineyard Gazette* to write an open letter to Katzenbach.

The letter, expressing shock at the testimony, called on Katzenbach to "stop playing the functionary and speak out against President Johnson's indefensible diplomacy of violence."

According to Buchwald:

The gut issue at stake was not the question of the right to dissent—most people agreed that dissent on Martha's Vineyard is a healthy thing, particularly during the rainy season—but rather, should people have the right to ruin a man's vacation by writing an open letter to the local newspaper on a subject that the poor official comes up to Martha's Vineyard to forget?

The pro-vacation people maintain that Martha's Vineyard should be considered a safe port-of-call for all those caught up in the storms of official controversy, while the pro-anti-Vietnam war factions on the island maintain that since Katzenbach spoiled their vacation by his testimony, they have every right to spoil his.

Tragically, the argument has split the island down the middle. Cocktail parties have become so acrimonious that hostesses are now asking their guests to wear life preservers at all times. Tennis games have taken on a new ferocity. Crews on the same sailboats are not speaking to each other and people are sneaking out at night and wrecking each other's sand castles.

It is hoped that some compromise can be worked out before next year. Cooler heads on the island feel that while Katzenbach has every right to defend his President's policies, he should refuse in the future to testify before the Senate Foreign Relations Committee during the month of August.

But so far nobody seems to want to compromise. The pro-Katzenbach people maintain that what the undersecretary of state says in Washington is his own affair and that he should not have to defend his statements on the beaches of Martha's Vineyard.

The anti-Katzenbach faction retorts by holding up a photo of the undersecretary and asking, "Would you buy a used vacation from this man?"

John's view of the ad, in the fullness of time:

"It has been fifty years and it still rankles. The fact was that everyone in our family, including my father, was against the war, but it was not as easy as announcing, 'Let's get out of Vietnam.' Of all the names on the list, the one that really gets me is Brustein in particular, head of the Yale School of Drama. I don't know why. Is taking an ad out in the *Gazette* really such a profound way of standing up for your opinions? And why pick out my father when there were plenty of other members of the administration and numerous editorial board types vacationing on the Vineyard? In his testimony on the Hill, my father told a bunch of lawyers in Congress that the Gulf of Tonkin Resolution was the legal equivalent of war, and they got angry because they hadn't understood or weren't smart enough to realize that was what they had voted for in the first place. Guys like Brustein, who, parenthetically, spent World War II on a merchant marine vessel, thought they were somehow taking a brave stand when it was pretty damn easy to be against the war at Yale."

To the degree that Nick and Lydia were hurt by the attack, they hid it.

After all, they had each other.

Like water seeking the right level, every couple finds its own way to happiness. One of the curiosities about the house is that despite the hard use it got in its heyday, there never was a dishwasher. John's parents claimed they love doing the dishes, finding the task romantic. She washed; he dried. If doing the dishes during their two weeks every summer on Martha's Vineyard was the secret glue, who were we to question their customs?

On a major anniversary, Mimi once made for her parents a hand-painted bowl in which she wrote their responses to the question: Why had their marriage lasted as long as it did?

She said the reason was he made her life possible.

He said it was the one thing he never needed a reason for.

Chapter Five

Summer Notes

From the beginning, the logs we ordered from A.G.A. Correa & Son in Maine—eight in all—were intended as more than just a simple guest register, although we never suspected how meaningful they would be. In the time since we began ordering them, the price has quintupled. Each clothbound volume is 8½ by 11 inches with two hundred interior pages made of 100 percent rag paper, which is considered as good a paper as money can buy. The canvas covers are a tasteful taupe.

In its product description, the manufacturer emphasizes that if you hold the paper up to the light, you can see the watermarks, and that the logs are often used by artists as drafting paper and by real-life navigators to record wind direction or to map a shoreline. The paper is "guaranteed not to bleed through, even with India ink," and on the spine is a small design consisting of two concentric circles with a vertical and horizontal line so that each volume is "readily recognizable on your bookshelf," a selling point emphasized on the company website along with the information that the design, called the Center of Effort, is a nautical term for a moment in physics similar to the sweet spot in a golf ball.

The company claims there was no reason to "worry about mildew or moisture. Our log is easy to maintain, and as impervious to weather as paper can be."

Judging from the number of nights various logs spent being drenched on the deck, we can testify to the accuracy of that statement.

At first we were self-conscious about defiling the pages of the ship's logs like the pang you get when you cut a ribbon on a present.

Then John's father broke the ice with an entry about the opening of the house:

The dogs and I arrived on the last ferry. Could not get the stove to work. I ate a can of cold chili and went to bed. Dogs ate raw hamburger—more acceptable to them than to me. Weather so-so. Pump still doesn't have a cut-off, but it appears to be half-installed and perhaps will be fixed by next week. But who knows? The wood stacked to the left is fully seasoned and should be used first. Boats are rigged. Outboard can be picked up, but they want two days' notice. Today is starting slowly, but should be okay. The trees have grown and another year gone by.

It is easy to picture him, awakening to the sound of gossiping geese, wearing his dress-down uniform of a holey shirt with baggy jeans cut off at the knees, pink calamine lotion smeared proactively on arms and legs, writing at the dark, frail servant's ironing table, the one that Lydia rescued from her family's camp in the Adirondacks. By waiting until after daybreak, he would not have to rely on the kerosene lamps for light, with their constant threat of calamity.

Another entry, typical in its simplicity:

There are compensations to getting older. I received a senior citizen shellfish license, no charge, never needs to be renewed, and good, I assume, until . . .

A code governed what went into the logs and what did not, an underlying censor that discouraged grocery lists and other daily drivel even though some squeaked by, such as "Empty lint panel on dryer; it is a fire hazard" or "Bottles and cans in Massachusetts are now returnable."

Many entries erred in the direction of glossing over the bad times, overemphasizing the good: photoshopping before there was photoshopping. Tributes were a mainstay: passages so purple, so rooted in the "oh flora, oh fauna" school of writing, that they constituted what one teenager called "clichéd cheesy blah," such as:

I'll never forget the way the ocean roared
Nor the way the delicate birds soared.

Getting to the island, and the relief that usually followed, was a common theme. At its worst the ferry was an equalizer, slow but dependable. Flying was not always an appealing alternative. From Anne:

Don't, as I did, sit directly in back of the pilot on one of those munchkin-size planes favored for midweek jaunts. Why? All I can say is that the feeling that overcame me was not confidence . . . as I watched the pilot pull a Swiss Army knife out of his pocket in order to fix the fuse that ran the landing gear. You get a very clear view of the house . . . which I did three times as the pilot fiddled with the wheels that were to determine our fate.

Recipes were acceptable: the food of summer, when abundance marries taste, is best of all. In the logs you will find instructions for my chicken fajita casserole (feeds thousands), Jamie Harrison's smoked bluefish dip, Ann Banks's painkillers (a drink), Amy Kaufman's Swiss chard risotto, Alex Auriema's mango salsa, Sioux Eagle's low-fat balsamic chicken, and the wild rice salad served at the memorial service for Linda Lewis. The aromatic thought of that salad, with feta and mint and pecans, brings back an image of the deceased's very young granddaughters, Miranda, Thea, Bea, Evie, Zoe, and Lily, at the outdoor service, whispering to themselves to be quiet as they tumbled in the scrappy grass. They seemed, as little girls so often do, otherworldly, composed of stares and sighs and somersaults. (A final grandchild, a boy named Jack, joined them a few years later.)

Clippings from the newspaper and drawings also welcome. Low expectations prevailed, as when a child dashed off some squiggles and a parent (me) promptly labeled them "waves."

The most common tone in the logs is one of pure praise, gleefully exaggerated.

I have never played so many games of gin rummy in my life. This is the way I want to live, and want to die.

One child wrote:

There's so much to do. Who needs TV, toasters, videos, and microwaves when you have the ocean, lots of books, the dirt road, flying horses, restaurants, the bike path, big waves, and the ferry?

Mimi's former husband, Jamie Harrison, wrote:

Two days of Vineyard's finest. Friday: a beautiful day at the beach with post-hurricane waves of six to eight feet making body-surfing feel more like tumbling. Dinner of swordfish, corn, and new potatoes. It can't get better. Early morning bluefishing. As easy as getting a dog to bark. Twenty-five in a morning and leaden arms and sunburned backs. If this is a dream I hope never to wake up.

Even when the fishing is terrible and more about hope than conquest, gratitude abounds:

I can think of no other place I'd rather go out and not catch fish.

If exclamation points are a form of verbal littering and if everyone should be limited to a lifetime supply of no more than twenty, the log is filled with the work of contributors who have exceeded their allocation, as in:

I love everything but the splinters!!!!!!!!!!!!!!!!!!!!!!!!!!!!!!!!!!!!

More tributes; these from children:

Martha's Vineyard has given me so many memories that I almost can't remember them all.

On Martha's Vineyard I am having the kind of childhood people used to have before I was born.

"Today is a historic day," began many of the entries, and it turns out that what constitutes History, that grand force of story-telling that pickles the past, was often in the eye of the beholder: who was finally old enough to drive the motorboat or go to mini-golf after dinner or able to catch minnows. "Last night," wrote my father-in-law, documenting his idea of a historic day, "I skunked Lydia in cribbage."

Tips:

Don't canoe home from the beach in the fog.

Just so you know: new kitchen faucets on backwards.

Avoid Alley's and up-island as much as possible: President's entourage creating havoc.

A surefire de-skunking formula:

Take ¼ cup baking soda, one quart three percent hydrogen peroxide, one teaspoon liquid soap. Mix all together and wet dog with solution. Let stand two or three minutes. Wash off. Hose best. It works.

TO THE NEW OWNERS

The secret to a long life for cut flowers:

Remove leaves below water line; change water daily; add aspirin to water.

Riddles:

Somewhere on this property a time capsule is hidden. Only four people know of its whereabouts, and they are sworn to silence. Its contents include crayons, various coins, a Ninja Turtle, and a plastic frog.

Warnings:

Active wasp nest outside sliding door to the back bedrooms. Other nest spotted above woodpile.

Beware: Rabbits with tularemia virus on the loose.

Lyme tick disease is Health Hazard for visitors and residents alike: rash, headache, fever, stiff neck, painful joints, and swollen jaws.

Pure silliness, such as a running list we made of new versions of the opening words of *Moby-Dick*:

- *Call me, Ishmael!*
- *You never call me, Ishmael.*
- *From now on, call me Ish.*

- *Ishmael never calls, never writes.*
- *Baked cod for dinner: fish meal.*

A reptile report, filed by John:

New snake. Kind of tan with spots. Has moved into storage shed.
Nick keeps wanting me to catch it so he can take it home as a pet.
I am beginning to run out of excuses. I tried telling him the snake
had already been caught, by virtue of its having taken up residence
in such close proximity. He did not fully accept this concept.

Random musings about guests:

Jeph Shaw is a nice boy, but how can you really admire someone
who failed "Flowers of the Alps" during his one semester abroad
at Tufts?

Celebrity arrivals are noted:

Arrived on the same plane as Jackie O. She had a scarf, an
umbrella, and some friends who picked her up on time.

Big moments and small ones are given equal billing in the
logs, including the time I apparently threatened to use the tick jar
as salad dressing, and some ungainly adult danced the "poodle-
reena," and group housekeeping efforts were performed to Maceo
Parker's "Pass the Peas." A few years ago, someone noted that my
son, Nick, "did the dishes once (which of course excuses him
forever! Well, he's cute)" and that John "through some terrible

error, surely not his own fault, locked Maddy's keys in her car. The upshot is that the locksmith can now find the Point." Justine and her babysitters Ashley and Sarah collected seashells by the seashore. One ravenous night in the early 1990s with many children in tow, we had a record-breaking table for twenty-three at the defunct Carolina's and a bill of $365 before the tip. A guest barely made a dent in her summer reading, *The House on Mango Street*.

Shopping sprees are recorded.

One summer we had a skinny cheerful boy named Matt with us before he set off for college. He had a duffel bag filled with books by the Beats and he bought his wardrobe for school from Take It Easy Baby in Oak Bluffs:

Three pairs heavy-duty green knee-length shorts	*$5 each*
One Navy captain's overcoat (black with gold buttons)	*$28*
One U.S. Army work shirt (black)	*$5*
One pair U.S. boots	*$10*
One African beanie	*$10*
One Danish Air Force hat	*$1.50*
In all, a lot of money.	

While Matt was computing his extravagance, John was sweeping the living area, muttering: "There is nothing in this world more destructive than sand and salt water; nothing."

Matt's response: "Right. That explains why the Allied forces relied on them so much during World War II."

I kept wondering: If I were in Matt's age group, how would I feel about the African beanie and the Danish Air Force hat?

Celebrity-sighting, no matter how fleeting or at how much of a distance, ranks as a popular pastime, birding without the binoculars.

Stars are everywhere. It won't be long before we see the birth announcements of Aquinnah Willis or Wampanoag Belushi in the gossip columns.

(In fact, Michael J. Fox named one of his twin daughters Aquinnah.)

In years past the island was a bastion of discretion, as this editorial entitled "Right to Privacy" from the *Gazette* dated June 4, 1985, makes clear:

It was news here the other day when King Hussein of Jordan and his family visited the Vineyard, and this was duly reported by the local newspapers. After all, kings don't drop by every week. What's interesting is why Hussein and his American wife should come here for a rest from the turmoil of the Middle East.

One guess, not to be too boastful, is that the Island has come to respect the privacy of people. The more famous they are, the more we leave them alone. Old secretaries of state and defense, former attorney generals, prominent newspaper columnists, publishers, editors all come here. And manage to get lost.

When director Mike Nichols (*The Graduate*) bought a home in the mid-1990s for $5.3 million, the *Gazette* not only published a front-page story, it also published an editorial about the impact such hefty sales would have on other real estate on the island. Nichols responded with this letter to the editor:

> What a lesson in irony. You have seen fit to put the purchase of Chip Chop on the front page of two issues and cap it with an editorial in a third. It will seem hilarious when I tell you that I have always cherished the Vineyard, to which I have been coming for 30 years, because of its New England restraint and sense of privacy.
>
> I suppose I should thank you since, partly because of your efforts, we have in recent days received offers for the property that far exceed what we paid. But we love the Island and look forward to becoming part of its community.
>
> We even love the *Gazette*. But if you don't stop yapping about this soon, I will turn the land into a beachfront parking lot and sell the house to Taco Bell. You have been warned.

Even celebrities must forsake their hideaways from time to time, and so over the years we have seen the actress Patricia Neal walking down Winter Street in Edgartown with a cane . . . Ted Kennedy at the Black Dog . . . Princess Di in Vineyard Haven . . . the Clintons at the airport . . . JFK Jr. buying a sandwich at Humphreys . . . Michelle Pfeiffer sunbathing . . . Meg Ryan dining . . . lawyer Alan Dershowitz on his cell phone at the nude beach at Lucy Vincent . . . Donald Trump docking a mega-yacht that could only belong to Donald Trump . . . Lady Bird Johnson . . . Henry Louis "Skip" Gates Jr. . . . Mike and Mary Wallace . . . Walter Cronkite . . . Harold Ramis . . . Larry David . . . Bill Murray . . . Caroline Kennedy.

You will find it takes an especially cunning eye to spot a famous person, because most are in mufti, wearing the same baggy cottons and flip-flops as everyone else. The first time I met our Vineyard neighbor, Anthony Lewis of the *New York Times*, I was convinced, judging from his ragamuffin outfit and the way he was scavenging what he referred to as "treasures" on the beach (sticks and shells and seaweed), that in fact he was someone caught in a delusion pretending to be Anthony Lewis of the *New York Times*. As a result, during our introductions, I made certain my tone was kind and gentle.

Many years later, in 2003, a guest and I ran into his second wife, Margie Marshall, on the same beach shortly after she, as head of the Massachusetts State Supreme Court, presided over a ruling that legalized gay marriage in the Commonwealth. If you knew Margie and Tony as a couple, you knew that her ruling was as much a reflection of their own union as well as a tribute to marriage in general:

> *"Marriage is a vital social institution. The exclusive commitment of two individuals to each other nurtures love and mutual support; it brings stability to our society. For those who choose to marry, and for their children, marriage provides an abundance of legal, financial, and social benefits. In return it imposes weighty legal, financial, and social obligations. . . . Marriage also bestows enormous private and social advantages on those who choose to marry. Civil marriage is at once a deeply personal commitment to another human being and a highly public celebration of the ideals of mutuality, companionship, intimacy, fidelity, and family. . . . Because it fulfills yearnings for security, safe haven, and connection that express our common humanity, civil marriage is an esteemed institution,*

and the decision whether and whom to marry is among life's momentous acts of self-definition."

The guest later wrote:

We had a really engrossing conversation. She really wasn't anticipating the uproar that followed it culminating (let us hope it's culminated) with George W. singling her out in his State of the Union address as an activist judge.

If you wish, you can spend your time on the island engaged in varsity socializing, but our mingling more often than not took the form of an egg toss at the birthday party for our neighbor's babysitter, or a memorial service for someone who died during the winter but whose family wanted summer as a backdrop for the tribute, or one of those peculiar Vineyard potlucks consisting of the leftovers of people about to leave the island, such as a single piece of pie, a tomato and a half, a peach, an inch of vodka, a box of grits.

Hollywood can, and does, glitz up the Vineyard with items like the following popping up in the *Gazette*: "Congratulations to Chilmark seasonal resident Tony Shalhoub, for winning an Emmy Award for best acting in the television comedy, *Monk*." Yet among the year-rounders there remains a family feeling in which loyalty wins out against glamour, as this bulletin indicates:

Oak Bluffs residents should know that sixth grade student Hannah Vanderlaske was recently hospitalized at Children's Hospital in Boston. Her recovery will be a lengthy one, and frequent trips to Boston are a must for the family—and an added burden to their expenses. Here is an opportunity to assist her family.

We also had our own private celebrities, the people we looked forward to seeing every year. Bob the Water Hero who fixed our well more than once, John the Propane Man who saved the day at 5:30 on a Saturday, the Bread Lady at the farmers' market who also sold delicious homemade granola.

More reports of creatures on the loose:

A mouse lives behind bookshelves. A bird has built a nest on the overhang part of the roof near middle bedroom. If you sleep back there she will knock on the window all night to scare you away from her babies. Raccoon stalks the porch at night. Seagulls on master bedroom roof.

From John's sister Anne:

Nature can be kind. Sudden evening thunderstorm leaves a dramatic orange sunset in its aftermath.

Nature can be cruel. And hard to stomach. Resident hawk seen eating the headless remains of gray/brown striped kitten in middle of dirt road. Large bird with mean streak.

Quotations are encouraged as a quick economical way to capture a memory or to fix a personality in verbal aspic. A card game played long ago by two little boys in which one said: "I may be cheating but you are cheating more so shut up." A teenaged boy, shouting from atop a Sunfish, "Do sailboats have brakes?" The same teenager when his alarm went off to roust him for work: "I hate waking up in the sevens. In fact, I hate waking up before the tens." That summer he ate a typical breakfast on the run before heading to work at Wheel Happy Bicycles in Edgartown: Wheat Thins dipped in hot sauce.

Three quotes are ascribed to me over and over: "Everyone has to write in the book" and "Why don't we all go and . . ." and "Come on. Every day is a beach day."

Milestones sometimes earn a quick but powerful nod, such as when Lydia saluted the birth of my son, Nick:

It's a boy. Champagne all around. A deep and resounding hurrah
for our small corner of the human race.

A few years later, Lydia on the arrival of Mimi's son, Avery:

Ten hours of labor, nothing but an aspirin at the end, reports baby
"already kind and pleased to be here."

Included for reasons that remain obscure:

August 4, 1992. One hundredth anniversary of Lizzie Borden's
stepmother's and father's death.

Advice is dispensed, from Flaubert:

"Spend! Be profligate! All great souls, that is to say, all good ones,
expend all their energies regardless of the cost. You must suffer and enjoy,
laugh, cry, love and work, in other words you must let every fiber of your
being thrill with life. That's the meaning of being human, I think . . ."

101

From Carol Shields:

"A person can go on and on tuned in to the daily music of food and work and weather and speech right up to the last minute, so that not a single thing gets lost."

Newfound thrills:

Attended the Chilmark flea market for the first time, and enjoyed the varied assortment of bric-a-brac and homemade goods. Stopped by Caffe Latte for a sampling of the best oatmeal and currant scones on the island . . .

Weddings:

In honor of the union of John's cousin Phelps Stokes Hawkins to Sandra Lea Earley, John's brother, Chris, wrote:

So much stands out. But surely the weather deserves first mention: "Would it rain?" was the question on all lips (or "Would it stop raining?" to be precise). Who could know, who could tell? Surely not the weather station, for days forecasting a warm and sunny Saturday, only to awaken to the awful, wet truth of clouds and drizzle. A desperate purchase of $80 worth of umbrellas was aborted at the last minute in the face of unwarranted optimism. A common refrain throughout the day: "I think the sky is getting a little light." But the sky was still dark as the groom and ushers had bourbon and ginger in preparation for the event. Wedding pictures: sky still dark at six p.m., the moment of the scheduled *wedding, the clouds parted, the sun shone, the rain became history, and the event began.*

Chilmark cops ended party. Too much noise. Final quote from Sandra: "I want to be in tomorrow's paper as a bride, not a felon."

Another wedding, this time described by Chris's wife, Kerry Stoebner:

That night, after the formal ceremony and luncheon, there was a bonfire and cookout on the beach. In the midst of all the festivities, Cotty [her four-year-old son] falls deeply in love with the bride and acts as her shadow for most of the evening. At the bonfire, Cotty insists that I tell Mia he doesn't like her anymore. I can only surmise that he feels slighted. Very reluctantly, I approach the bride with Cotty in tow. She greets him warmly and insists that he sit by her by the fire. He then turns to me and insists that I ask Mia whether she loves him. Knowing no shame I do my son's bidding. Mia is dumbstruck and a heavy silence falls. Momentarily she recovers and with open arms says, "Of course I do." A noble performance by Mia. Cotty spent the rest of the evening by her side until he was too tired to stay awake. When asked later what was special about Mia, what drew him to her, Cotty acknowledged that the white dress had something to do with it but he also stressed, "She understands."

If only all our interactions could be that perfect and that simple: *She understands.*

The artful complaint is a mainstay, diatribes about hardships offered in a tone of near hysteria in the apparent belief that because you are on vacation you should never have to deal with burst pipes or with empty propane tanks or with hauling trash to the landfill. Often the complaints are about the weather:

> *As we near the end of our ten-day stay one question haunts us, plagues us, keeps us up at night: What, we wonder, would it have been like if the sun had shone? Torrents of rain and wind so forceful even the ticks have run for cover.*

Anne, among the more prolific and polished writers in the log, once filled an entire page with the same sentence over and over: "I will not complain about the opening of the house."

Another lively report came from a friend named Richard Halgin, author of *the* college textbook on abnormal psych, with his own abnormal desire to see the world entirely on cruise ships. He even served for a time as a member of the editorial board of *Porthole Cruise* magazine, not "Peephole," as he was careful to remind us. He saw the house as one big ocean liner:

> *I am pleased to award the SS Katzenbach a 5-star rating, which is reserved for only the finest of world-class vessels. Our captain must be congratulated for his leadership and overall management of the ship, and the Cruise Director [that would be me] kept all passengers occupied in the most creative onboard activities, especially walking in muck to the ocean. The dining chefs are masters, and the dining room itself was the setting of refined elegance, although I would prefer Waterford Crystal*

rather than paper cups and fine linen napkins although the Marcel is quite colorful.

In their haphazard eloquence, the logs attested to the truth that everyone's Vineyard is different.

Our version of the island followed a simple script.

Errands when necessary.

Fishing: often. Fish: never, or almost never. (Now I need the sad-face emoticon.)

Trips to Oak Bluffs for the Flying Horses and Mad Martha's for ice cream when the children and their cousins and friends were young.

For company, we preferred repeat customers who knew the drill: a steady diet of lassitude and self-direction raised to the level of an art. Breakfast and lunch were self-serve, and how you spent the day was entirely up to you, usually a combination of swimming, walking, sailing, kayaking, biking, golfing, reading, writing, chatting, napping followed by a feast of some stripe in the evening.

We had little in the way of noisemakers. No television ever, though sometimes you could hear the scratchy voice of an announcer at Fenway on a barely functioning portable radio.

Nighttime: books, poker, stargazing, storytelling.

Most islanders have a favorite seafood market. Ours was John's in Vineyard Haven, where we had a charge account and I liked to check in with the owner, a dark-haired woman named Sandy, who always asked about my in-laws, especially after they became too frail to visit the island. Sandy's deep voice was somewhat at odds with her affable attitude, a miracle given that she worked nonstop in the summer months until her recent retirement.

We almost never went to restaurants so we never had any to recommend.

I walked endlessly, forced marches with a uniquely selected band of friends bonded at the very least by a similar zeal for impassioned ambulation. The walking cure: that's my motto. I have been told that from a distance, I had the aspect of one of those mean officers with a Gallic sneer in an antique black-and-white French Foreign Legion film, taunting his charges, "Move, you dogs, or die." On a good day, I would walk or jog the four-plus miles to the main road and back, then walk to the ocean on the dirt road and by the water another two miles, and after swimming, walk from the cut up the beach to Long Point and to the saltwater pond, at least another couple of miles, round-trip.

For some, the island was one huge nature fix: they knew that if birds are diving in the water, a school of fish is swimming beneath, and they knew what a north wind means and what a southwesterly wind means as well. They have combed the sixty acres of the Polly Hill Arboretum. They have signed up for kayak tours of Tisbury Great Pond, and for snake and turtle tours at the Felix Neck Wildlife Sanctuary, and for birding expeditions with Susan Whiting in order to hear about brown thrashers with their apparently impressive repertoire and to discover the differences among juvenile sanderlings and semipalmated plovers and ruddy turnstones. They embrace everything about the natural world, even "rocks and hurricanes," as one deceased islander liked to say.

Someone else was entranced by the llamas at various farms on the island, and she once pasted into the log a brochure of "Llama Facts" to answer frequently asked questions regarding these members of the camel family, who are primarily beasts of burden, with a life span of about fifteen to twenty years and an average weight of 280 to 450 pounds. This person, quoting the brochure, claimed that llamas are intelligent and easy to train, and that their grease-free, lightweight wool is warm and luxurious. We also learned that llama stomachs have three parts; they communicate through a series of ear, body, and tail postures; and spitting is their way to say, *Bug off.*

Some guests wanted to go on erosion tours. One stunning example is the Wasque Reservation, which has lost forty of two hundred acres to ocean waves that have guzzled cliffs, forests, and even parking lots. One house, a fifth of a mile from the ocean when it was built in 1984, is now about twenty-five feet from a cliff. The owners have removed the furniture and the propane tank and are hoping for the best. Another house, built in 2007, was moved intact—including the bowling alley, movie theater, and main house (which weighed 1,200 tons)—230 feet away from the edge in the summer of 2013.

Other guests preferred organized events: gospel music in the tabernacle at Oak Bluffs, concerts of sea songs, the Fourth of July parade, the antiques show in Edgartown, the annual road race in Chilmark, music at the Hot Tin Roof, ghost tours of Edgartown and Oak Bluffs. Someone else liked yoga: hot yoga, yoga for osteoporosis, yoga in the grass, yoga in an exquisite place, yoga on a paddleboard (though not on a kayak, at least not yet). She also inhabited an artist's Vineyard and knew all the people who dyed cloth and made paper and blew glass.

A neighbor spent her time volunteering at the Dumptique, the shed at the landfill where you can drop off and/or acquire castoffs. Her house had hand-carved wooden birds and a landscaped lawn, but she seemed most joyful when orchestrating rags and trinkets.

Another neighbor loved to "shop" at the Dumptique and later report on the value of her loot:

> *A copy of* Loose Change *by Sara Davidson, SKU 76993641; Hardcover; First edition; used, good condition/no dust jacket/ beginning to yellow; retails on Amazon.com for $2.11 plus shipping costs.*

Anne's husband, Steve, took on the shed and its level of hygiene and organization as one of the unsung challenges in all his visits.

You could hear him mumbling, "Eleven-year-old phone book." *Thump.*

"Splintered oar." *Thump.*

"Leaky bucket." *Thump.*

Mostly, he liked to take it easy.

Steve wrote the most laconic log entry ever:

> *Pump works.*
> *I don't.*

Little kids lived for catching crabs and for naming them, in the demented belief that crabs have true pet potential. They schemed to get the brass ring at the merry-go-round in Oak Bluffs or to sleep on the top bunk. Young teens lived for the video arcade in Oak Bluffs and later for driving around, trolling for other members of the adolescent tribe. One summer we were plagued—or was it blessed?—when a group of the teenaged girls (Justine, Jen, and Claire) showed an unwavering infatuation with a certain all-male a cappella group called Vineyard Sound. Founded in 1992 by students from Wesleyan, Connecticut College, and Skidmore, the group, which has expanded to include members from many mostly East Coast schools, provides concerts all over the island, all summer long. Dressed in pastel shirts, ties, shorts or khakis, the performers specialize in a range of songs from "Southern Cross" to "Zombie Jamboree," which were two of the selections at the best party ever on Thumb Point, when Lydia turned eighty.

I always brought a stack of books. When Marilynne Robinson's *Gilead* came out, Lydia and I were tripping over each other as we agreed about its delights and subtleties.

Lydia's mini-review:

Who would have thought it possible? The voice of God throughout. It was brilliantly written, so much so that the context and the content barely mattered. To think that the author was able to keep the voice of the minister completely authentic throughout. A remarkable feat, as I was waiting, even hoping, perhaps she'd slip up so I could chortle, ahah!!!

Someone tore about ten pages out of one of the logs, the jagged edges of the remnants looking like shark's teeth, not the most consoling image. Their absence remains a mystery: Who wrote what to cause such a savage gesture of regret?

From time to time, we reread entries from friends who vanished from our lives and wondered: Where did friendship flee? Did it hide its head amid the cloud of stars above or did it go to some creepy warehouse for lost connections between people? What happened to the couple with twin toddlers whose rocky marriage came along with their luggage and their double stroller, to the child who had only one trick (shoving jellyfish down people's bathing suits), to the woman whose idea of vacation began and ended with a bottle of Bombay Sapphire gin and who conscripted her daughter at every turn to bring her drinks while she sat on a lounge chair reading a Tom Clancy novel? Where are they now? Most likely at their own summerhouses, entertaining their own guests who in turn will disappear into the dunes of time, kidnapped by the gods of memory.

The logs helped us recollect the small details and also the big themes: the Summer of All Fog, the Summer of the Board Games, the Summer of Hurricane Bob, the summer when Timmy Murphy, a friend of my son Nick, landed in jail for a couple of hours for having trespassed on Jim Belushi's property by (somewhat) total mistake in the dark in the middle of the night, the summer of Phil's first visit, the Summer of Obama fund-raisers, the summer when the stranger drowned in the cut, the summer when Kay died, the summer of Lydia's eightieth. Thanks to the logs the muddle of time was less muddled.

Eventually, we ordered new books. "The Ghost of Thumb Point" was changed to "The Host of Thumb Point" when some-one's then young son was frightened by the word "ghost": his mom blotted out the G and then tortured the h into becoming a capital letter. In an effort to keep the peace, Lydia volunteered to be the ghost, saying she would be happy, when the time came, to come back and haunt everybody. You had to admire this woman.

"Pug Haiku and Poodle Prose" was a natural title, given how much the Katzenbachs loved their dogs. I was the one who did the ordering, and I recall feeling on edge about the possibly sacrilegious connotations of "A Lobster Named God" and of "Boiling the Pope and Other Vineyard Recipes." When the salesperson at A.G.A. Correa & Son sounded flummoxed—"'Boiling the Pope'? Are you sure?"—I assured her: "It's the family's favorite casserole, heavy on the monkfish."

"Sounds delicious," she said politely.

We kept other potential titles in a kind of mental layaway. I liked "Boats against the Current" (literary!) and "Never Write the Ending," the latter expression for Lydia's belief that bleak moments often yield to better fates in the fullness of time, a conviction she often shared with her patients and which I have adopted as yet another mantra. Someone suggested "Idyll Speculations" or "What Is This Property Actually Worth?" We also considered "Famous Vineyard Curses" and "Oh, Well" in honor of the summer when there was no water.

(The Summer with No Water: not *all* our memories are pristine. We arrived on the island one day where we were met at the ferry by 'ohn's parents as they were leaving. His dad warned us that we would be facing "typical Vineyard problems," which, we discovered later when we tried to fix dinner, translated to no water at the house. First we called "the well guy," who arrived early in the morning and (a) got the pumped fixed, (b) left, and (c) came back the next day and redid everything when we complained that instead of water, brown sludge emerged from the faucets. It was August during a drought, and part of the problem was that because the house lay low by the pond, it was hard to get a generous flow of water. Even when we did have water, it was often brackish though it always tested as potable. The well was now sucking up sand and mud from the bottom, so our savior dug down even more, saving the day and the vacation, but the event underscored for us just how fragile Thumb Point was ecologically.)

Sometimes when my children and their cousins were little, I would fast-forward and imagine them tall and grown, friends I hoped, maybe at the same colleges, in each other's weddings, coming to the island with their own children, the cousins and second cousins, quarreling with their own stubborn toddlers about the necessity of wearing life jackets in the cut, and then the vision would vanish, unsubstantial, false and silly. I would be drawn back into the current of the dense present, back on duty, with the light on and the flag up, supervising après-beach snacks of chips and sliced apples or searching for tweezers as I nattered on about how people didn't listen, because if people did listen people would know better than to go barefoot on the deck, and wondering who removed the aspirin from its proper place in the green unit in the living room. And so the days blurred and blended. Without these books, who would ever remember anything about what happened where or when or to whom? I am so grateful we persisted in taking notes on ourselves. In a culture that worships the delete button, there was something comforting about the indelibility of these words. Much of what appeared was unguarded and sometimes even dull, but, oddly, that was part of the appeal. The logs were a tribute to what is best about summer, its power to lull, its essential sleepiness. We took photos too, of sand mummies and of dune-diving and of people cavorting in the surf wearing that universal expression of pure yikes, but words are images too, and in this house they counted just as much.

Chapter Six

The *Jaws* Effect

Today we think of it as the playground of presidents and movie stars, so it may be hard to believe but Martha's Vineyard used to be a well-kept secret, a lonely postscript to the Cape, favored by people with an ornery streak because it was such a pain to get to: Who wanted to take a ferry—all that waiting and all that bother—when you could simply drive down Route 6 and land in Wellfleet or Truro or Provincetown?

A tragic accident in 1969, the release of a movie in 1975, and a series of presidential visits, beginning with Bill Clinton and his family in 1993, changed the profile of the island forever.

The accident occurred in the summer of Woodstock, the moon landing, and Manson, on Chappaquiddick, known as "Chappy," an island across the harbor in Edgartown. With a year-round population of about two hundred, and a small convenience store that is open from time to time, it feels like a secret. Its residents call Edgartown "the mainland."

Ted Kennedy, the senator from Massachusetts, spent the night of July 18, 1969, partying with a group of young women, known as the "boiler-room girls," who had worked in the presidential campaign of his brother Robert. They gathered with Kennedy and some of his aides a year after Robert Kennedy's assassination to renew ties and to lament the horror of events of the preceding year. Ted Kennedy left the festivities in an Oldsmobile at around eleven at night with twenty-eight-year-old Mary Jo Kopechne. Shortly afterward, his car drove off Dyke Bridge, a wooden platform without guardrails, and sunk into the water. He escaped from the mostly submerged vehicle and, dazed and drenched, he ended up (the stories vary as to how) crossing the harbor into Edgartown sometime between midnight and dawn, claiming to have swum across despite a bad back. Mary Jo Kopechne was later found in the backseat of the car, drowned, after the pocket of air, to which she had apparently scrambled, gave out. A cartoon at the time showed the car with its trunk barely poking out of the water with a license plate that read: FUTURE PRESIDENTIAL PROSPECTS.

During an inquest, he denied being drunk at the time of the accident.

> **The Court:** Were you at any time that evening under the influence of alcohol?
>
> **The Witness:** Absolutely not.
>
> **The Court:** Did you imbibe in any narcotic drugs that evening?
>
> **The Witness:** Absolutely not.
>
> **The Court:** Did anyone at the party to your knowledge?
>
> **The Witness:** No, absolutely not.

The Court: In your opinion were you sober at the time
that you operated the motor vehicle to the Dyke
Bridge?

The Witness: Absolutely sober.

On the day that Kennedy pled guilty to leaving the scene
of an accident, he addressed the citizens of the Commonwealth:

There is no truth, no truth whatever, to the widely circu-
lated suspicions of immoral conduct that have been leveled
at my behavior and hers regarding that evening. There has
never been a private relationship between us of any kind.
I know of nothing in Mary Jo's conduct on that or any
other occasion—and the same is true of the other girls at
that party—that would lend any substance to such ugly
speculation about their character. Nor was I driving under
the influence of liquor.

Little over one mile away, the car that I was driving
on an unlit road went off a narrow bridge which had no
guard rails and was built on a left angle to the road. The
car overturned in a deep pond and immediately filled with
water. I remember thinking as the cold water rushed in
around my head that I was for certain drowning. Then
water entered my lungs and I actually felt the sensation of
drowning. But somehow I struggled to the surface alive.

I made immediate and repeated efforts to save Mary
Jo by diving into the strong and murky current, but suc-
ceeded only in increasing my state of utter exhaustion
and alarm. My conduct and conversations during the next

several hours, to the extent that I can remember them, make no sense to me at all.

Although my doctors informed me that I suffered a cerebral concussion, as well as shock, I do not seek to escape responsibility for my actions by placing the blame either on the physical and emotional trauma brought on by the accident, or on anyone else.

I regard as indefensible the fact that I did not report the accident to the police immediately.

Instead of looking directly for a telephone after lying exhausted in the grass for an undetermined time, I walked back to the cottage where the party was being held and requested the help of two friends, my cousin Joseph Gargan and Paul Markham, and directed them to return immediately to the scene with me—this was sometime after midnight—in order to undertake a new effort to dive down and locate Miss Kopechne. Their strenuous efforts, undertaken at some risk to their own lives, also proved futile . . .

Instructing Gargan and Markham not to alarm Mary Jo's friends that night, I had them take me to the ferry crossing. The ferry having shut down for the night, I suddenly jumped into the water and impulsively swam across, nearly drowning once again in the effort, and returned to my hotel about 2:00 a.m.—and collapsed in my room. I remember going out at one point and saying something to the room clerk.

Then he asked the citizens of the state to decide his fate.

The people of this State, the State which sent John Quincy Adams, and Daniel Webster, and Charles Sumner, and Henry Cabot Lodge, and John Kennedy to the United States Senate are entitled to representation in that body by men who inspire their utmost confidence. For this reason, I would understand full well why some might think it right for me to resign. For me, this will be a difficult decision to make.

It has been seven years since my first election to the Senate. You and I share many memories—some of them have been glorious, some have been very sad. The opportunity to work with you and serve Massachusetts has made my life worthwhile.

And so I ask you tonight, the people of Massachusetts, to think this through with me. In facing this decision, I seek your advice and opinion. In making it, I seek your prayers—for this is a decision that I will have finally to make on my own.

Kennedy eventually was given a suspended sentence of two months in jail.

In the years that followed, Ted Kennedy stayed in office. His public persona prospered, but his personal life was a wreck. His wife, Joan, who suffered her third miscarriage soon after the incident, left him, and for years he pursued a reckless besotted social life until finally settling down in 1992, when he married his second wife. The story of the scandal resurfaced during each of Kennedy's presidential bids and left him mute during the 1991 confirmation hearings for Supreme Court justice Clarence Thomas, who was charged with sexual harassment by Anita Hill. Kennedy died in 2009.

As much as Chappaquiddick drew attention to the Vineyard, the book and the movie *Jaws* bear even more responsibility for the island's fame. Peter Benchley had been mulling the idea of a shark frightening a resort community for years, carrying in his wallet a newspaper clipping about a 4,500-pound shark that had been captured off the coast of Long Island in 1964 to prove to any potential publishers that the story was not so preposterous: it had an antecedent in the real world of fact.

Benchley kept a running list of possible titles, each clunkier than the next, including "The Edge of Gloom," "Leviathan Rising," and "Tiburon." He also envisioned "Jaws of . . . Despair, Anguish, Terror" (take your pick), shortening it at the last minute to the one-word wonder by which the book became world-famous.

When Benchley wrote the novel, he considered himself a failure. He and his family had moved from New York City to Pennington, New Jersey, which his research revealed was the least expensive town in the tristate area where one could still reasonably commute to the city. With mortgage payments and tuition looming, the advance of $7,500 sounded good.

"The great fish moved silently through the night water, propelled by short sweeps of its crescent tail." From its opening words on, the book is curious to read both in how dated it is in a way the movie is not and also in light of how the movie improved on the text.

Upon publication, *Jaws* was not universally praised: one critic called the novel "very cookie-cutter—almost no shark and way too many character conflicts. It just reeks of a first novel where the writer did not really have a voice yet."

Set in the fictional town of Amity, Long Island, it was written in an era when it was considered risqué to describe housewives as filled with secret longing, such as in the following passage from the point of view of Police Chief Brody; observe in particular the phrase in parenthesis:

> The pay was fair: $9,000 to start, $15,000 after fifteen years, plus fringes. Police work offered security, regular hours, and the chance for some fun—not just thumping unruly kids or collaring drunks, but solving burglaries, trying to catch the occasional rapist (the summer before, a black gardener had raped seven rich white women, not one of whom would appear in court to testify against him), and—on a slightly more elevated plane—the opportunity to become a respected, contributing member of the community.

Much later, a character explains how bad it will be for Amity if it loses all its summer business to shark attacks, with yet more race-based asides:

> "The town survives on its summer people . . . Call it parasitic, if you will, but that's the way it is. The host animal comes every summer, and Amity feeds on it furiously, pulling every bit of sustenance it can before the host leaves again after Labor Day. Take away the host animal, and we're like dog ticks with no dog to feed on. We starve. At the least—the very least—next winter is going to be the worst in the history of this town. We're going to have so

119

many people on the dole that Amity will look like Harlem." He chuckled. "Harlem-by-the-Sea."

The hardcover version of *Jaws* stayed on the bestseller list for forty-four weeks. Benchley sold the paperback rights for $575,000 and the movie rights to Richard Zanuck and David Brown for $150,000.

Benchley had summered (ah, that quintessential New England verb) on Nantucket and knew the Vineyard, but at first Zanuck was hesitant about filming on the East Coast in a community where rich summer people live, sensitive to the notion that he wouldn't want his own privacy in a rich enclave jeopardized in a similar way. Hollywood usually goes to Northern California to film scenes set in New England, but even back then most of the beaches had high-rises and the filmmakers wanted a more authentic retro look. When scouts saw the Vineyard, they were sold. Menemsha, in particular, delivered in the Department of Authenticity. (Still does.)

When Zanuck and Brown hired Steven Spielberg as director, he was only twenty-six years old, yet he had achieved critical success with a TV movie called *Duel*, about a deranged truck driver stalking a car, and *The Sugarland Express*, a feature film starring Goldie Hawn. A story is told that Spielberg initially thought the script, based on the title, concerned dentistry, and after reading it, he said, "Wow, this is like a movie I just made about a truck and a driver. *Jaws* and *Duel* both have four letters, they're both about a leviathan going after man." So much for first impressions.

In order to avoid tourist season, the director filmed in May and June when the waters are still cold, one reason the swimmers are seen fleeing the water with such dispatch.

During the filming, Spielberg quickly sensed how the island and its inhabitants could all be characters. Locals were folded into crowd scenes and even dramatic roles whenever possible. Carpenters and construction workers built a fisherman's shack for Quint, the bounty hunter, to live in and a dock that would disintegrate in one of the more frightening scenes. The island became as invested in the film as the film was in the island, with many schoolchildren recruited as extras for the beach scenes and also for small speaking roles. In a recent interview with the *New York Times*, Spielberg talked about the agony of making the movie, of running over budget and going entire days without a decent shot: "It's a fear of getting lost. And then staying lost in a quagmire of having made a bad choice and now I'm stuck with it for the next 60 days of shooting. I felt that way on 'Jaws' only because it was so hard to make, not because I didn't know how to make it. I was lost."

The final product reflected none of the struggle, and when the movie was released in the summer of 1975, viewers embraced it. All the flaws in the book disappeared and all its strengths emerged. The movie was a slimmed-down version of the novel: gone was an elaborate and cringe-inducing love triangle between the police chief and his wife and the marine biologist. Quint shows up very late in the novel—on page 231. In the movie Quint appears in early scenes, growling at the townspeople, reciting off-color ditties, not yet center stage but definitely in the picture—a force to behold.

Jaws was the celluloid equivalent of a riptide, flinging the viewer into deep scary waters, a classic story with one of the oldest and most durable plots: a stranger comes to town and nothing stays the same. In its wake, life imitated art. Not just a stranger came to town, but a deluge of strangers descended, having discovered the island initially through the eyes of Quint and Hooper (the oceanographer from Woods Hole) and Brody (the police chief).

As long as viewers ignored the creature from the deep and concentrated on the fantastic vistas, the film was a chamber of commerce windfall. To this day, in yet another of the island hierarchies, anyone who can claim an association with the movie in any aspect whatsoever is automatically bathed in a flattering light. When the film's cinematographer put his house, briefly, on the market in the summer of 2015, his *Jaws* pedigree was part of the sales pitch.

A few years back, Netflix staged an outdoor viewing of the movie attended by more than a thousand people accompanied by a trivia contest:

"Which Martha's Vineyard town features the storefront used as Amity Hardware?"

"Edgartown."

"How many replica sharks were made, and how much did each shark cost?"

"Three, costing $250,000 each."

"What was the name of the ship that Quint sailed on in World War II?"

"USS *Indianapolis*."

It is not as if, pre-*Jaws*, the island was bereft of people of fame and consequence, but in earlier times most relished their role as hermits. Remember Jackie Kennedy Onassis and her evening rituals: *Dinner: fish or meat, salad, a glass of wine. And she required a fire in her bedroom fireplace no matter what the weather.* Think of the editorial in the *Gazette* titled "Right to Privacy," about all the prominent people gladly huddled in their hideaways. Summon, also, the image of Anthony Lewis in his dress-down clam diggers, scavenging for "treasures" on the beach. The atmosphere on the island changed slowly. By the early 1990s, when the Clintons decided to vacation on the Vineyard, pictures ran worldwide of Hillary buying a straw hat in Vineyard Haven and Chelsea at the fair and the former president on the links with his political adviser Vernon Jordan.

The Clintons' first visit garnered fawning coverage in the two newspapers islanders revere most: the *New York Times* ("In Its Staid Way, Island Is Agog Over Clinton") and the *Vineyard Gazette* ("Clinton Weather Forecast: As Fair and as Warm as the Island").

The *Times* quoted Steven Rattner, an investment banker and summer resident: "I haven't seen so many serious people atwitter since I lived in London during the royal wedding."

Vernon Jordan and his wife, Ann, hosted a forty-seventh birthday dinner for the president, taking into account Chelsea's allergy to shellfish, Hillary's aversion to heavy sauces, and the president's to flowers (thus topiaries with grapes served as the centerpiece). The menu differed from the former president's current vegan regimen.

Hors d'oeuvres: island littlenecks and oysters with mignonette and cocktail sauce, mini codfish cakes, tomato vinaigrette tarts, and smoked bluefish crostini with horseradish mayonnaise. Appetizer: corn pudding with maple-syrup-glazed Smithfield ham and beefsteak coulis followed by a salad of island tomatoes with buffalo mozzarella and cilantro pesto. The entrée: grilled harpooned local swordfish, served with tiny new potatoes with minted virgin olive oil and grilled baby island vegetables with Japanese vinaigrette.

Dessert: lemon poppy seed birthday cake with island blackberry coulis and blackberries and Chilmark chocolates.

For that first visit, the Clintons decided to stay at the home of Robert McNamara, a simple house compared with many of today's extravagant dwellings, in what was interpreted as a gesture of generational détente. During McNamara's tenure as secretary of defense, the war in Vietnam escalated, making him the target of much of the antiwar fervor.

McNamara kept a low profile on the island, quietly supporting a variety of worthy causes. In 1972, when he was assaulted during a nighttime crossing of the ferry, he refused to make a public scene. A columnist in the *Gazette* described what happened this way:

> Mr. McNamara was standing at the lunch counter on the upper deck of the *Islander* when someone called his name. He went to the door. In the darkness a voice said there was a telephone call for him in the wheelhouse aft. Mr. McNamara, who was expecting a call from his wife, started walking across the windy deck. Somebody grabbed at him and tried, says Sanford Ungar [a reporter at the *Washington Post*], to push him overboard.
>
> Mr. McNamara thrust the assailant away, having either lost or not lost his glasses in the course of the waltzing—a detail that depends on who's telling the story—and went back to the lunchroom. No charges were filed. The Federal Bureau of Investigation decided it didn't qualify as a federal case. The Steamship Authority filed a description of the incident with the state police.

The assailant, it turned out, was a twenty-six-year-old island resident who was angry at McNamara not about the war, but because of his purchase of a tract of land that included a nude beach that would no longer be available to bathers.

A special section of the *Gazette* alerted Bill Clinton to the golf course options, which include the Farm Neck Golf Club in Oak Bluffs, the Edgartown Golf Club, and the Mink Meadows Golf Club in Vineyard Haven. At Farm Neck, he was warned that holes one, four, and twelve were all bedeviling, each in a different way, but that the views were worth the frustration.

Afterward, some of the towns realized how hard hit they would be by overtime hours in providing security details for the president, but as Oak Bluffs police chief George Fisher put it, "Our whole goal is to put the sunny side up on Martha's Vineyard . . . I think it's marvelous. We haven't had a presidential visit here in a very long time." Ulysses S. Grant was the first president to visit, in 1874.

The floodgates opened.

More princesses, more movie directors and CEOs and TV stars and anchorpeople and novelists and journalists and artists.

New visitors were attracted to the island for the same reasons old visitors were.

Plus, the added joy: each other.

The coverage for the initial Barack Obama visit in 2009 was as breathless as for the Clintons, though as the island had become more accustomed to these intrusions, the reporting was a little less starstruck. "Presidential Vacation Winds Down" ran a headline on page eight of the *Gazette* in 2014 during our last summer, declaring that Obama's vacation was interrupted three times by unfolding events at home and abroad, including problems in Iraq and Ferguson, Missouri, and the murder of journalist James Foley, causing him to return to Washington, D.C., and to issue public statements while on the island. Otherwise, he had a low-key time, biking with his family (properly helmeted), dining at Atria, and hitting the links at Farm Neck five times.

One of the most obvious changes on the island is ease of access.

The days of leaving your car wherever you wished in Woods Hole and counting on standby vanished, the process hastened when, in the summer of 1995, word got out among predominantly black college students and recent grads that a good time could be had in the historically African American town of Oak Bluffs, and hundreds arrived to celebrate the Fourth of July, many without reservations, taking advantage of the Steamship Authority's same-day standby guarantee, crowding the beaches and taxing the island's hospitality.

From an AP story by Katharine Webster:

Martha's Vineyard is becoming paradise crowded, and the resort island is struggling to cope. As the Labor Day weekend approaches, restaurants, hotels and shops are looking forward to a crush of visitors—mostly black college students and young professionals—who spend lots of money. But other residents and long-time summer vacationers anticipate nightmarish ferry lines, raucous parties and a general disturbance of the peace that draws them to this island refuge.

Sometime before the turn of the century, a few black Boston families took the train and the ferry to Martha's Vineyard each summer for the Baptist tent revivals. Then they began to stay the entire summer. Thus began the Highlands neighborhood in Cottage City, which is now Oak Bluffs—one of the oldest, most desirable vacation spots for black Americans.

That community helped give the island a reputation for racial harmony, helping draw even more black Americans to all three island towns on Memorial Day, July Fourth and Labor Day. The crowds include family vacationers with local ties and young people who come in search of good times. This summer, mixed in with the tensions between the newer visitors and old-timers has been some racial friction. The conflicts came into sharp focus over the July Fourth weekend, when people with ferry reservations couldn't get to their boats and Oak Bluffs' main street turned into a giant party every night. "We came for July Fourth for a birthday party for a friend of ours. We'll never do that again," said Steve Douglas, who has brought his family from Medford to the Vineyard the past 15 summers. "It's the college kids coming down," Douglas said as he relaxed at a beach popular with blacks nicknamed "The Inkwell." "It's like spring break in Florida."

Or Virginia Beach, one white summer resident of nearby Edgartown charged in a letter to the *Vineyard Gazette.*

In that Virginia city, black fraternities used to organize a "Greekfest" on Labor Day weekends. But in 1989, when a mostly white, helmeted police force tried to break up the throng on the boardwalk, fights and looting followed.

Joseph Passafiume's letter called on authorities to "take back the Vineyard" from an "invasion" of "hoodlums" who were drawn by ads in Jet and Ebony magazines. The magazines denied running any ads, and the newspaper received a flood of replies calling Passafiume a racist.

Passafiume did not return phone messages. But his wife, Margaret, said up to 1,000 people came to a party in a rental house across the street from her family's summer home. And in the house next door there were parties every night where they played "vulgar black music," she said.

"It's called the 'black weekend,' and it is really an invasion," she said. "They were very rude, they swore, they urinated anywhere they could. They went on people's property, parked their cars anywhere they wanted, and down on South Beach it was trashed."

That's not how Richard Bell remembers it. The white, retired Methodist minister, who lives a stone's throw from Circuit Avenue, Oak Bluffs' main street, said the only problem was a lack of parking. "I don't think there's any racial trouble," he said. "They're all welcome."

Some events of this past July 4th weekend—the biggest ever—may lead to changes in police and ferry policies.

On that Friday night, cars waiting for standby room on the ferries from Cape Cod led to a nearly two-mile traffic backup. Many regular visitors with ferry reservations missed their boats, and one or two scuffles broke out at the ferry terminal parking lot.

Circuit Avenue turned into a party zone. Some visitors brought in a truck loaded with ear-rattling speakers. Others dispensed squeeze bottles of liquor from car trunks to the roughly 1,800 people who couldn't fit into the dance clubs, bars and restaurants.

Merchants and police say most visitors were polite and friendly. Only 19 people were arrested over six days.

Sgt. David Roberts, who commands only eight full-time Oak Bluffs patrol officers, worries that his force isn't trained to deal with large crowds. His officers are reinforced during peak weekends by a few state troopers on motorcycles and horseback.

He also worries about the potential for racial violence. "We have had incidents in the past that have caused us some concern . . . like hit-and-run accidents," he said. "We're concerned that one incident like that could get things out of hand."

After that, the rules changed, and now car reservations are made months in advance, starting as early as January for summer visits. The motive for the change in policy was cited by some as racially motivated and discriminatory: Why only after a bunch of young blacks showed up did the Steamship Authority need stricter regulations? Or was it self-preservationist—does any resort community really want to get known for beach blanket bingo? Or was it simply a matter of time before a more elaborate system would be needed, and the time happened to coincide with this influx of young people? For many, no matter what, it was not a shining moment.

After 9/11, any lingering element of ferry casualness vanished.

In terms of real estate, prices rise and fall in waves. Between 1997 and 2001, high-end property grew at a rate of roughly 40 percent a year. Around that time, I had dinner at the home of two friends who had rented a three-bedroom house near Vineyard Haven in which two of the bedrooms were in the mildewed basement. It was on the market for $1.7 million; its water view consisted of a shard of something possibly liquid and possibly rippling in the far distance. It probably goes for twice as much today.

The Martha's Vineyard Land Bank Commission began in 1986 with a mission to conserve land and to keep it open to the public from "sunrise to sundown," except during the hunting season. So far, about 3,100 acres are conserved, about 5 percent of land area on the island. The conservation movement was partly motivated by the heady 1980s building boom and partly by changing island habits. The commission's view of the state of affairs that inspired the land bank in the first place:

> Martha's Vineyard Island has witnessed unprecedented change in the most recent decades. Farming declined; centuries-old pastures and fields were left to knot into vines and shrubs. The "freedom to roam" was curtailed as fences were erected across trails, beaches were gated off and hunting was restricted.

Money to buy land comes from a 2 percent surcharge on most real estate transfers—land, house, beach lot time-shares, for example.

The land bank has declared the shortage of affordable housing on the island to be "a public policy dilemma of significant proportions," but its role is to assist other groups that have been chartered to develop affordable housing.

It is not a cheap place to live: the Martha's Vineyard Housing Needs Assessment (2013) reports the home price is 54 percent above the state median and the island weekly wage is 71 percent of the state average. In spring 2016, Realtor.com advertised a "starter home" (three bedrooms, three baths, 1,352 square feet, .32 acres) for $495,000.

The "Island Shuffle," an annual ritual, involves moving out of a winter rental to make way for the summer crowd. Long-term renters can face sudden disruption when a house is sold. One popular librarian, confronted with that scenario, chose to leave her job and the island. Stories circulate of people pitching tents, living in cars, couch surfing, and sneaking into vacant seasonal houses.

To add to the sense of dislocation and futility, many of the best beaches are private. A cartoon in the *New Yorker* that showed a police officer as he questions two would-be beach-goers with the caption, "Sorry, folks, but I need to see your tax returns," resonated sufficiently for someone to post it in one of our logs. Massachusetts law stipulates that anyone carrying a fishing pole has access to any beach at the high-water mark, but on the island the welcome wagon for the odd goodwilled angler is not always in evidence, especially on the gated beaches such as Quansoo and Black Point, where a key has been priced as high as $415,000. An article in the *Boston Globe* by Donovan Slack in the summer of 2005 questioned the wisdom of the purchase:

> What do you get for your money? At Quansoo, it is a deed for 1/77th of a 1-mile stretch of white sand and dune grass and a high-tech key. Plus, there's a property tax bill of $539 and annual association dues of about $150.

One of the most predictable trajectories on the island is that of the person who lobbies fiercely for variances in order to build a house and then becomes, once the house is in place, an environmental zealot who would never grant such a variance to anyone else. The No Trespassing signs may be hand-hewed and tasteful, fashioned, in the case of one homeowner, with the words stenciled on a weathered oar, but the point is the same: *I got mine and I don't want you to think it's yours.*

Real estate being lust and guilt by the square foot, you hear the stories of other people's windfalls with barely concealed envy. The best deal I ever heard about was of the couple who paid one dollar for several prime-time water view acres up in windswept Aquinnah during the 1930s because the wife in the family who lived next door was lonely and wanted neighbors.

These days, the asking price for the most expensive houses has been purposely omitted from ads and is available only upon request.

Recently I heard an exchange between a boy of about six or seven and his father, who was doing his best to ignore the child as he flung himself on the bench where the man sat glued to his cell phone outside a store in Vineyard Haven: "But I don't want to go to your movie locations. It's boring. Why can't you understand? Talk to me, Daddy." The boy's father, absorbed in his mobile device, said he couldn't have a civilized conversation if the child kept whining. It struck me as what you might hear on the New Vineyard, as opposed to the Old Vineyard, which exists as a kind of misty-eyed platonic ideal of Kindly Year-Rounders and Grateful Summer Guests coexisting in perfect harmony with a minimum of traffic and a plentitude of just-caught fish.

Every year an annual community fund-raiser, now called the Art Buchwald Possible Dreams Auction after its former emcee, attracts a large and generous audience. The event benefits Martha's Vineyard Community Services, which includes the Island Counseling Center; CONNECT to End Violence, a domestic violence and rape crisis center providing free and confidential services; and Island Wide Youth Collaborative, as well as administers early childhood programs such as Head Start and childcare services, education and support through the Martha's Vineyard Family Center, and disability services. The agency also runs the Thrift Shop on Chicken Alley in Vineyard Haven.

The donors, generally summer residents, offer dinner with themselves or sunset cruises on their yachts or a tour of their workplace or a walk-on part in their television show in exchange for as much money as the "dream" will generate. In that sense, the auction is the model of a certain kind of thrift in that it feeds the celebrities' vanity and the coffers of various island charities both at once. One year JFK Jr. offered to escort the high bidder on a bike tour of the island. Christopher Reeve let someone copilot his private plane. The chance to get Carly Simon to sing at your private party was so popular that she agreed to sing at two different events, doubling the contribution. In 1994 alone, she brought in $160,000. Katharine Graham routinely hosted successful bidders for lunch in the executive dining room at the *Washington Post*, preceded by a tour of the building. More recently, you could bid on "Sushi with Belushi" or a geneology session during dinner with Henry Louis Gates Jr. as well as vacations in France, Italy, and Scotland. In 2015, the auction raised almost a half million dollars, with hefty prices paid for a set visit to *Late Night with Seth Meyers*, an afternoon with artist Allen Whiting, and two vacations in a private home in Galway Bay, Ireland. Someone paid $12,000 to sail to Nantucket with writers Geraldine Brooks and Tony Horwitz, with signed copies of their work as a bonus. The comedian Jimmy Tingle replaced Buchwald in 2013, saying he was humbled to be the successor of a man who as an orphan was raised in foster homes and who joined the Marines before finishing high school. He then spent his adult life grateful to the people and institutions that made his success possible and on the island paid it forward at the annual charity event urging his fellow Vineyarders to "give til it hurts." Tingle said, "Art Buchwald was a hero to me and many other writers and comics for a number of reasons, but primarily because he could be funny in print. Making people laugh from the stage is hard to do but making people laugh from the page is even harder. One reason is most people aren't drinking while they're reading."

To see how much the island has changed, consider what the Possible Dreams Auction was like in 1979, its first year.

Someone paid $45 dollars for the privilege of pretending to be a crew member on the ferry. For $35 dollars, someone else got to spend the afternoon as an air traffic controller. It cost David Boyd $85 dollars to dance with Carly Simon at the Hot Tin Roof. A sail with Walter Cronkite raised $225. Other items: a fur-lined jacket worn by Mia Farrow in one of her movies, tips from an expert on how to winterize your home without ruining its character, and an apparently much-coveted lesson in the little-known art of seaweed collage.

Chapter Seven

Operating Instructions

We never rented the house formally, but we often gave away time in it to family friends and even virtual strangers. One summer one of John's sisters chose to give her two weeks as a gift to a contractor and his family who had helped her remodel a house.

John and I drafted this note to give him and his family a basic sense of the lay of the land, and the water:

> *We hope you and yours are getting psyched. We suspect you will have a fine time on the island.*
>
> *Here are a few details you should be aware of.*
>
> *Directions:*
>
> *Not sure whether you're coming into Vineyard Haven or Oak Bluffs. Regardless, you want to head over to the south side of the island and . . .*

136

TO THE NEW OWNERS

In the interests of not revealing the precise address, let's just say the rest of the directions include such landmarks as the afore-mentioned dips in the road, mailboxes, forks, etc. We also included a pep talk:

You are going to travel a total of 2.2 miles on this dirt road. It meanders around. Be persistent. Be confident . . . At the top of the hill BEAR LEFT. Continue past other houses. Watch for sandy spots. The house will either be open, or there will be a key on the shelf of the outdoor shower (facing the house, on the extreme right). That key will open all doors.

It might make sense to invest in an island map. It's very easy to get turned around and have trouble finding the right dirt road, especially at night . . . I think there's a map on the bookshelf in the LR. Poke around.

A word to the wise: Take a load of groceries out there if pos-sible. There is a Stop & Shop in Edgartown (cheapest . . . except nothing *is cheap on the island). In Vineyard Haven and in West Tisbury there are Cronig's (significantly more expensive, but very popular with the people who don't like chain stores). There's a Stop & Shop by the Vineyard Haven ferry also.*

Fish: Go to John's Fish Market in Vineyard Haven. If Sandy is there, say you're staying out at our place. She's an original. Take her advice as to what is best. Some people swear by Poole's down in Menemsha, but we prefer John's and not because of the name.

Vegetables: Many locations. Morning Glory Farm just outside of Edgartown seems the best.

Eat island pies: There is a kiosk just outside West Tis-bury called Eileen Blake's [since closed down]. Not cheap, but absolutely primo. *There are many other bakeries on the island, all with unique character and specialties, but her pies are by far the best. But you can get a good chocolate chip cookie all over the place.*

At the house: Three kayaks and one motorboat. The fuel for the motorboat will either be in it, or up in the storeroom (just past the outdoor shower). It's a four-stroke, so NO oil mixed in with the fuel. Everyone wears life jackets in the boats! When there is a SW wind, it can sometimes pick up (this is pretty obvious), which makes getting to the beach a wet adventure.

Getting to the beach: Beware of the shallows. Essentially, you head directly across the pond. You will see other boats gathered on the sand. Just head there. With the kids, please be alert to undertow. Once you get to the beach, plop down anywhere.

IF THE CUT IS OPEN . . . The cut is a channel from the pond to the ocean which is opened about three times per year. It salinates the pond. It creates a wonderful place for the kids to play. But it has a darker side: It creates sandbars that stretch from the beach out nearly 100 yards. The currents on the edges of the bars can be dangerously strong, so make sure that kids are always being watched. As benign and happy and beautiful a beach as it is—and you won't see many that are better in your life—it's still the Atlantic and waves can pick up from day to day and undertow can be harsh. Make sure the kids keep their eyes out for seals; they seem to like watching the swimmers. They bob up and down, looking like sea dogs.

If the kids are into crabbing, there are nets in the storeroom. If the cut is open, it acts like a magnet for bluefish and stripers.

Late day into the night and very early a.m. are the best times. There are two spinning rods assembled (one right hand, one left) in the living room. Feel free to use those. There are other rods and reels disassembled in the middle bedroom, left-hand side of the house. Fishing lures are in a blue fishing bag in the top storage bin in that room. There are also some waders hanging in that closet. If you go fishing, bring flashlights, and remember, they call bluefish choppers for a reason. Grab them behind the head and avoid their teeth if you want to keep your fingertips. Unlike some fish, they see very well out of the water. You've been warned. Stripers can be lipped easily. Just avoid the dorsal fin, which is very sharp.

    Other spots to fish: It's a haul, but if you can, head up to Aquinnah. Either Philbin Beach (look for the rock outcroppings) or the Menemsha Basin. Or Menemsha Pond itself: there are always people working the jetty. Again, low-light conditions. Dusk. Outgoing tide. Night.

    You will see fly-fishing stuff. If someone wants to use it, have them call first, so we can explain the drill. Stripping baskets, night time, what flies, how far to wade.

    Need to rinse gear off with water after a couple of uses. You can always stop in at Larry's (across from the Edgartown Stop & Shop) next to Al's Package Store (another valuable resource) or at Coop's (on the way into Edgartown . . . look for the yellow mailbox on the left).

    Speaking of water. We are on our own well. Sometimes when it has been very dry, the taste of the water gets brackish. We always use lots of store-bought spring water.

    The kitchenware and tableware are a mishmash of stuff collected over the years. There is a brown chest in the LR which holds extra threadbare ratty towels and sheets. Anything can go to the beach. The washer and dryer are self-explanatory, but try not to overburden them. There's a gas grill on the deck behind the kitchen. It's seen better days but still works valiantly. Just keep an eye on it when you're cooking. It would be terrific if you managed not to burn the place down.

Kids' rooms on the right, next to the outdoor shower. The rooms get HOT in the daytime, so keep fans on and windows open.

In the LR there is a green chest of drawers filled with the sort of miscellaneous stuff you will need. There's a splinter removal kit in there (or, at least, there should be). The deck gets someone every year. Also: the oyster shells in the pond can slice a foot pretty easily. We always wear some sort of water shoes. On the other hand, our kids do not, and have no scars yet to speak of. This is luck.

There's horseback riding, water ponds to swim in, all sorts of stuff. Check the Vineyard Gazette *and* Vineyard Times *for other activities.*

Watch out for Lyme-carrying ticks. Unfortunately, the ticks you can see aren't the ones that carry the disease. But if you find any, or either variety, just take a small jar, fill it with dishwasher soap, and drop them in. Cruel death, but necessary.

There are two new couches being delivered for the LR. They should be there by the time you arrive, or so says Maine Cottage furniture . . . we'll see.

Beware of opening the skylights and forgetting about them during a rainstorm. This has happened to many houseguests.

TO THE NEW OWNERS

It's a funky place, very much a beach house, and a bit battered and worn—but very special. If you are in doubt about anything, err on the side of having fun. Like I said, don't hesitate to call. The phone at the house is 508-696-XXXX. We have Verizon's cheapest plan, so if you need to call Beijing, best to use a cell. Don't be dismayed about the spotty coverage out there, especially for computers. It's just the way things are.

Lots to explore. Try to avoid the main towns in the afternoons. They can be jammed with people.

One last thing: garbage. We recycle glass, plastic, and paper. You will see a trash can or two as you pull up by the propane tanks. Make sure you seal anything up in there effectively, otherwise you will invite every raccoon and skunk on the Point to dinner. Also, in the heat, the stuff inside gets very *funky* very *fast. Trash and recycling goes to the same place: closest/easiest is the Edgartown landfill, which is located just past the airport entrance (heading east) and before the left-hand turn to Vineyard Haven and Oak Bluffs. Pull up to the kiosk and pay the guy. They only charge for the barrels of trash. A couple of bucks for each. You will see folks recycling madly, and then tossing trash bags. It's pretty obvious what to do. The landfill hours are listed in the Vineyard phone book by the phone (naturally . . .). Don't let stuff accumulate too much—this is advice everyone gets but roundly ignores. There are gloves in the drawer where we keep trash bags. The wicker basket that holds trash in the kitchen eats the bags, so double-bagging is wise. Also for the aforementioned skunks.*

If someone gets skunked—well, there's always tomato juice. Wise to keep some on hand. There's some dog "Skunk-off" which people have used in the green bureau. Check the logs for our surefire formula. We've never been nailed, but had a couple of nervous close calls.

Any questions, let us know. Have a great time!

Chapter Eight
The Ideal Guest

Being a guest isn't easy: all those hoops and hurdles that can only be divined upon arrival. You go to someone's house and discover that if you are not willing to gush over their photo albums from every cruise they ever took, with twice the enthusiasm for shots of them at the captain's table, or to listen to their seven-year-old play the violin for hours on end, or to volunteer in the kitchen only to court bloody knuckles grating cheese all afternoon, you may have exceeded your welcome before you even experienced it.

Our hoops and hurdles were transparent.

At its most irritating, the island is all about schlepping, especially during the high season when the roads are overrun with SUVs, so it was a godsend when a guest volunteered to pick up the papers on the morning grocery run. It was equally important not to complain about supplies or the lack of them ("What?! No soy milk?"). Given the location of the house in relation to the beach, it didn't work to lament the rigors of the journey as if rowing over in a soulful canoe or paddling over in a biceps-building kayak constituted hardship. In a world filled with troopers and princesses, the latter were advised to vacation elsewhere. One of our most challenging guests said he was allergic to the ocean, causing another guest to ask: "Which part? The salt or the water?"

In the logs and in our heads we kept a list of attributes for the ideal guest, who should:

(1) Share our passion for baseball.
During the summer of 1995, all we could think about was whether Cal Ripken Jr. should play his 2,131st game on September 6 in Baltimore, dethroning Lou Gehrig, the New York Yankees legend, or should he let sleeping legends lie. According to his manager, Earl Weaver, Cal Ripken is a steady working-class sort of guy. "He loves baseball so much, taking ground balls, hitting, competing—that's relaxation. Cal's such a creature of routine. I don't know what he'd do if he took a day off. It might mess him up for months. I don't know and I don't intend to find out. People shouldn't be complaining because this guy wants to earn his paycheck every night. He should be a national hero." Anne, writing in the log, asked if he attained this landmark did it mean he would get Cal Ripken Jr.'s disease? It is the kind of joke that Justine, when she was a little girl, put in the puzzling category of something only grown-ups laugh at.

Preferably, our guests rooted for the Red Sox, though this was not a deal-breaker as John's sister Anne is a Yankees fan—a weak link in the bloodline. If you muttered the words "October 27, 2004" within her earshot, she would cock her head and say: "No problem. Every team deserves to win once in a century. It would be ungracious to deny its fans that one small pleasure. Now if your guys could just win twenty-five more, we'd have something to talk about." (After 2007, and again after 2013, Anne became a touch less staunch in her superiority.)

(2) Be willing to clean.
The house was a sand magnet, so anyone willing to wield a broom was likely to receive a return invitation. On rainy days, help was always welcome as we examined the spices and the other long-term foods for expiration dates, speculating that the thyme had probably changed plant phylum while sitting on the shelf for ten years and how the garlic powder was "like Gibraltar" before being pitched.

(3) Leave the house ready for your next guests.
Never leave garbage for someone else to take to the dump, but if you are forced to do so, because, for instance, you are my sister-in-law Anne and you can't find your pug anywhere, a groveling note is a complete necessity:

> *My sincere and most humble apologies for not making a last run to the dump. I know I left stinky, maggot-ridden garbage and am going to spend the entire hellishly hot, long, traffic-choked drive back to New York thinking of a suitable penance (i.e., being made to sit through a Red Sox–Braves Worlds Series game and forced to cheer for the Sox).*

Anne often contributed poetry, including "A Remembrance of Repasts Past," a screed against leftovers:

Last Thursday night for dinner
We had a lovely meal
All the best and freshest food
Amazing in appeal.

We couldn't bear to toss it
And see it go to waste
Knew that you would appreciate
Even a little taste.

Perhaps you won't arrive
Just when you said you would
We're sure sole in beurre blanc sauce
Will reheat just as good.

This poem serves to remind
That food, it tends to spoil
Leave it in your memory
Not in the fridge, in foil.

(4) Obey the rules of the dirt road.
If someone pulled off to the side to give you the right of way, it
was bad form not to "wave your gratitude," though if your car was
full and everyone was waving too wildly, it could be mistaken for
sarcasm, so we suggested that good judgment guide the degree of
enthusiasm. I envied the perfection of my neighbor's papal wave:
one hand raised upright, palm facing out, moving in a slow, dignified horizontal arc of recognition.

(5) Understand that we are far from stores.

In fact the walkability rating on websites is zero because it is at least three miles to get a newspaper or a cup of coffee, with nothing but forest in between.

(6) Write in the guest log.

One of our favorite contributors was Leslie Ware, a longtime editor at *Consumer Reports*, who often visited along with her husband, Phil Caputo. As part of her job she was often engaged as a tester of various products. When she judged olive oil, she decided the term "extra virgin" is meaningless on domestic labels and that what you want to avoid is an elusive but unpleasant characteristic known as "fustiness." She used her magazine's trademark style of nitpicking objectivity to describe the property. Her first of many entries:

> *A beach house must be on or adjacent to at least 100 feet of crushed sand, with water in the distance. It must be a walled structure with a roof and, preferably, wooden shingles that have turned brownish from exposure to aforementioned water. Our panel of staffers journeyed all over for the quintessential beach house. We found a clear winner.*

Each visit, she subjected the house to the magazine's famous rating system, weighing in on precipitation, quality of the surf, and sunshine-to-rain ratios.

She once gave our vista the high rating of a full black circle, while labeling the Grand Canyon "yawn," Yosemite "snore," and

Yellowstone "blah." Her dry humor was the functional equivalent of a hostess gift.

CONSUMER REPORTS RATES THE BEACH HOUSE 1998
Primo moonrise: Reddish.
"Kissed by a cherry," says Maddy.
"Due to refracted light," says Phil.

CONSUMER REPORTS RATES THE BEACH HOUSE 2000
For our annual (except for 1999) report on the nation's beach house, Leslie Ware, Phil Caputo, and an English setter tested the Katzenbachs' residence. Our testers spent 3.89 days in the residence, shifting between two different rooms. Average temperature: 68.7° F. Total rainfall: 10" (all during a 5-minute period). Total number of fish caught: 0. That's zero. Nada. Zip. As usual. Overall we've rated the Katzenbach beach house a CR Best Buy. John and Maddy deliver excellent room and board for a reasonable fee (all you gotta do is write in this book).

CONSUMER REPORTS RATES THE BEACH HOUSE 2001
Fishing: What can I say? The providers let their women down again. Instead of a striped bass, the fishermen caught two dozen sugar doughnuts.

CONSUMER REPORT RATES THE BEACH HOUSE 2002
Fishing: Nothing, not even an anchovy.

CONSUMER REPORTS RATES THE BEACH HOUSE 2003

Once again, our tester showed up at the Katzenbach residence.
Invited? Mooching? Who knows at this point?
　　Conveyances: Unacceptable.
　　Zodiac motor: Gave out just as Justine and company crossed
the sidebar. Paddling was necessary.
　　Volvo hose: Spritzed radiator fluid, prompting the guys to
make repairs and Maddy to say, "I don't trust this f—r anymore!"
　　Sunfish: A problematic grommet lowers our rating.
　　Double kayak: Disappeared.
　　Canoe: It works!
　　Bumper sticker spotted on State Road:
　　　　STOP MAD COWBOY DISEASE
　　　　DEFEAT BUSH IN '04

CONSUMER REPORTS RATES THE BEACH HOUSE 2004

Fishing: Poor. We have lost any memory of what a real, whole
fish looks like.
　　Consumer Reports: *We are* very *popular, having been asked*
to research a car for Justine (good in snow, but cute), a car for
someone else (big but green), vacuum cleaner for Ann Banks
($500 but bagless).

CONSUMER REPORTS RATES THE BEACH HOUSE 2005

Weather: Bee-you-tee-full as we say in our Yonkers, New York,
headquarters.
　　Fish had two categories that year:
　　(1) Catching: None. All of us are shocked!

(2) Eating: Phil's swordfish roll-ups, with lots of chopping by his lovely acolytes, Claire ("How do you chop an onion?") and Justine (a cucina expert from her time in Italia).

CONSUMER REPORTS RATES THE BEACH HOUSE 2007

Fishing: Holy mackerel! Phil actually hooked and brought home a striped bass (silver and blue), 29 inches, no 31, no 32, 33 . . . whatever. The manly men grilled it, and it was good and true.

CONSUMER REPORTS RATES THE BEACH HOUSE 2008

Because print journalism is dead, we have moved online. For our full report, go on to: www.C.R.Katzenbach/fun.house@ MV.org.

Best overheard quote, from Ann Banks, on the deck, to Phil: "Don't you think human beings are hardwired for transcendence?"

Phil to Ann: "Yes, but we also seem to be hardwired for wars about whose transcendence is best."

(7) Either like dogs, or pretend to.

(See Chapter 9 for details.)

(8) Enter our dumb contests.

After all, the beach is filled with competition: first in the water, first in the boat to arrive back at the house, first in the shower. Who gets the first blueberry pancake? Who spies the house first as we round the corner on the long road?

One summer we sponsored the First and Only Vineyard Fog Contest, with prizes for the best one-line description of fog and the worse.

"Fog is like gray butter."

"Fog is the revenge of a rainbow that got ignored."

"Fog is a cloud in need of a face-lift."

"Fog is a serial killer of sunsets."

"Fog is a lot better when one knows where they are."

"Fog is grief without borders."

"Fog is God's gift to nudists."

"Fog is golf, spelled backwards, almost."

"Fog coming in across the pond is like the ghosts of Confederate soldiers on parade." (Could work in either category, according to the contestant.)

"Fog is what happens when the clouds don't use birth control . . . rain's soft-bellied cousin . . . the number one vacation destination of old memories . . . Fog is the childhood I am glad I never had . . . a stealth missile without the explosions . . . devours the dawn like peanuts . . . the sky, with poor reception . . . a rumor of doom."

"Fog is God's smoke ring."

"Fog is the bad breath of angels."

"Fog is combed clouds."

Called in by a departing guest on her cell from Route 495: "Fog is like an old dog lying in the hallway, loudly berated, quietly loved."

"Fog is the ocean's labyrinth." Same caller.

"Fog is eviscerated pillows." (She really wanted to win.)

Finally, from John's sister Anne: "Fog is a substance that turns more or less useful humans into nothing but bad poets."

I asked a professor then at Mount Holyoke College, Mary Jo Salter, the author of five books of poetry and an editor of *The Norton Anthology of Poetry* and now at Johns Hopkins, to judge the entries. She picked "the sky, with poor reception" as the best and "gray butter" as the worst, which she called "really disgusting." When I told her that both were mine, making the contest seem, I acknowledge, rigged, even though, if you looked at it objectively, the victory and the defeat cancel each other out, she sent me this note:

> *Her counsel asserts, to avoid even the appearance of impropriety, that Ms. Salter was like totally clueless when she chose the best and the worst definitions, because she had like no idea that Ms. B, her friend and walking companion in the early morning hours when we all know there is often fog, wrote them. It's kind of poetic that Ms. B wrote both. She wrote the best of lines, she wrote the worst of lines, like fog, which we can all agree, except when we don't, is wishy-washy.*

Undeterred, I announced a new competition:

"If the sun made a sound when it set, what would it be?"

To which our judge answered, "Like a cracked egg landing on a frying pan? Do I win? After all I've done for you?" I informed her that not only did she win, but that also she had offered such a memorable and stirring line that the only reasonable plan of action was for the contest to begin and end with her contribution.

(9) Show appreciation.

Kurt Vonnegut used to tell a story about an elderly uncle who would be sitting under an apple tree, chatting, sipping lemonade, and then "would suddenly interrupt the agreeable blather to exclaim, 'If this isn't nice, I don't know what is.'" Vonnegut loved this saying and used to urge people to "please notice when you are happy."

Chapter Nine

Mister Ulf, Famous Writer

All families subject newcomers to secret tests, but in the case of the Katzenbachs the test is not so secret: you are measured almost entirely on your willingness to allow dogs to jump all over you and to slobber while acting as if this is the most fun you can imagine. The more cheerfully you submit to fleas and fur and drool, the more welcomed you are.

Dogs occupy a special level of citizenship in my husband's family, a higher order of being than most mere humans. This was not necessarily my view, but as a soldierly daughter-in-law I learned to keep my opinions on this subject under wraps and to listen to the many stories of dog escapades, especially as they relate to dogs on the Vineyard, in a seeming state of enraptured attention. I understood that when you marry a person, you also marry their pets and their pet anecdotes.

The dog of the hour when I first met John's family was a St. Bernard named Beowulf.

There was a reasonable expectation, given his girth, that Beowulf would guard the house and protect it from intruders. Indeed, he often slept lying against the front door, 180 pounds of pure supine bulk. His days must have been innocent as his evenings showed none of the disturbed dreams one associated with insomnia, guilt, and dread.

He slept like a rock.

Visitors would enter the house by applying leverage to Beo's sleeping form, never once waking him as they gained entry by sliding his comatose form across the floor and then nudging him back to his place of sentry.

By day, Beo was huge. And hungry.

Left unattended, he liked to swoop his tongue onto the dining room table and could swallow a stick of butter all at once. One time I saw John's father feeding him a big dish of leftover steak of excellent quality and realized that another difference between his family and mine was that there was no such thing as excellent leftover steak in mine. When I commented to John, out of earshot of his father—I did not want to appear impolite—that this might be considered a waste of good food, John alluded to his father's POW experience. Part of the joy of not dying was to live with a sense of plenty such that you were able to feed your dogs whatever you damn well want.

In the case of Beowulf, the pleasure must have been doubled considering his apparent intelligence.

Years ago, matchbook covers contained many enticements for betterment. You simply had to fill out the form and send it in the mail, and who knows what windfall might come your way: better penmanship . . . sales opportunities . . . acceptance at a third-rate military academy for teens was a strong possibility.

At one point, John's father and Anthony Lewis enrolled Beo in the Famous Writers School, a mail-order business that encouraged applicants to think of themselves as potentially gifted writers. The ads contained testimonials, with names and photos, from satisfied students:

"Your course made it possible for me to sell six articles to *Woman's Day* for $2,050."

"I submitted my . . . column to the Santa Cruz paper and it's been running ever since."

"My article was published in the *New York Times* and later exhibited at the World's Fair."

The promotional literature pointed to legendary successes: a quarter-million-dollar movie deal, a $100,000 book advance. The school also published a magazine with articles about how to write a novel in half-hour segments and advice on "where and when to use anecdotes."

All you had to do was take a test, and if your work showed "evidence of writing aptitude" you would be offered the chance to enroll.

Beowulf's two sponsors filled out the application as if he himself had answered the sample questions:

The sun rose in the sky today like . . . *a St. Bernard.*

The dark and stormy night reminded the traveler of . . . *a St. Bernard.*

A smile lit up her face like . . . *a St. Bernard.*

These answers and a dozen more exactly like them, equally breathtaking in their rhetorical leaps and their dazzling ingenuity, showed such promise that Mr. Beo W. Ulf was indeed accepted at the school. He received a customized form letter of congratulations suggesting that with hard work and regular tuition payments, he too was bound for glory.

One day a personal sales rep from the company arrived at the family home in Riverdale to collect tuition, and he was greeted by Beo, supine as usual, and by John's sister Anne. She said Mr. Ulf was not at home at the moment, taking pains not to mention Beo's full name while he lay there the whole time doing what he liked best, sleeping.

After Beo, John's parents had many other dogs: standard poodles, including Lailie and Sam and Belle and Willie, and a mixed-breed rescue dog named Jazz. John's parents put what might be called extreme pressure on me to do anything only twice: in both cases, to get dogs. Our first poodle was called Bullet because I finally agreed to bite the bullet and get a dog. We liked the name because it was counterintuitive: a poodle named Bullet is like a pit bull named Tofu. Bullet proved to be a well-chosen name because it invited so many variations on a theme: Bullerina when the dog was graceful, Bul-letdown when he did something bad, Bull's-eye when he caught a tennis ball in his mouth. His ashes are now buried on the property, as are those of his successor, Porsha, a brown female, also with a demanding temperament.

Bullet's accomplishments during his first visit to the island: learned to swim (and, in turn, learned that poodle fur, when wet, is very heavy), ate sushi (he found a bluefish carcass on the beach and devoured a disgustingly large portion), barked at fog, barked at shadows, barked at a skunk, learned that all water is not necessarily good to drink (like salty pond water), displayed a decided preference for sleeping on the wicker sofa with white Haitian cotton cushions.

One time Lydia left a note in the futile hope of curbing canine indulgence.

I have bought a new quilt for the "master" bed. Expensive, natural, and I love it, so please treat with care: e.g., no dogs, poodles, pups, pugs, whatever, on it or furniture. If you cannot control animal species, put a large towel on furniture.

To which Anne responded,

Sorry. Pugs can't read.

But apparently they could write, and not only could they write, but their entries in the log demonstrated what my friend Mary Jo, the fog contest judge, calls a "high haiku IQ."

Anne's dog Dayzee was especially prolific:

HOPE
Is that a biscuit?
That thing right there in your hand?
Oh, I thought it was.

EDGARTOWN
When I'm on the town
The people love to touch me.
Why not? I'm pretty.

MY PROBLEM

It makes me throw up.
But I can't stop doing it.
I love to eat sand.

RAISON DU CHIEN

Do not ask me why.
You would never understand.
My job is barking.

MANIFESTO

I am on the couch.
In comfort and defiance.
I am on the couch.

MAY HAVE BEEN WRITTEN BY MY MASTER ANNE

Late in the season
I'm glad I'm a Yankees fan.
Don't you wish you were?

AGENDA

I am sleeping here.
And when I am done with that,
I'll be sleeping there.

SHOPPING

We're going shopping.
But I must wait in the car.
This is just plain wrong.

But no matter how proud the family members are of their pets and their genius as writers, no one ever scaled the heights achieved by that old slobbering St. Bernard, thanks to the Famous Writers School.

Homer.

Dante.

Chaucer.

Shakespeare.

Milton.

Ulf.

Chapter Ten

Phil

Every summerhouse has, or should have, *the guest* who returns year after year, without whom summer would not quite be summer.

Phil Caputo visited for several days for many summers, at first by himself and soon with his wife, Leslie Ware, not only a longtime editor at *Consumer Reports*, but also a confident sailor and an old-fashioned WASP Democrat. Our children were never sure where Phil and Leslie fit in the family, except that they had been part of the summer landscape for so long that no one questioned whether they would visit, just when. Justine called him un-Uncle Phil.

John first met Phil in Florida, when he interviewed him for a profile in *Tropic*, the Sunday magazine of the *Miami Herald*. They became friends after the article appeared, which made only gentle mention of the more problematic aspects of that time in Phil's life.

Phil was at the peak of his roué days and his literary fame, having broken into fiction after writing what is widely considered one of the best memoirs about Vietnam, *A Rumor of War*. On the dust jacket from one of his books published in that era, Phil is pictured wearing a shiny shirt of Qiana—a thankfully no longer popular slippery-feeling synthetic fabric—with a gold chain resting (I am sure he hoped provocatively) on a slightly exposed chest. A quote from *A Rumor of War*, spoken by a commanding officer, appears in the sixteenth edition of *Bartlett's Familiar Quotations*: "You're going to learn that one of the most brutal things in the world is your average nineteen-year-old American boy."

Phil likes to say that he went to Vietnam *because* he had a happy childhood, growing up in a generation of boys who loved John Wayne and all the World War II movies, and who chafed against his safe suburban childhood. In college, he joined the Marine Corps version of ROTC. After graduation, commissioned as an officer, he was sent to guard the air base in Da Nang. Months into his tour, disillusioned by the heat, the killings of an amorphous enemy, and the loss of his own men, he found himself feeling murderous rages. After the war he became a conflict reporter, traveling all over the world, seeking something—not quite solace, not quite enlightenment—in witnessing horrors and filing stories about them. From 1980 to 1985, he was caught in a perpetual dark night, which took the form of drug and alcohol abuse, two failed marriages, and a less than robust sense of what it meant to be a parent to his two sons.

John interviewed Phil as he was emerging from those times. "There's no such thing as an ex-Marine, and I don't think there's such a thing as an ex-Catholic." By the time I met Phil, he had recently met Leslie and he had calmed down considerably. He began going to Mass. He took comfort in the words of the ancient philosophers, especially Marcus Aurelius, who counsels "resignation without despair." All along he kept himself in good condition, swimming a thousand yards several times a week and working out in the gym so that even today, he conveys indisputable strength.

If you ask Phil which of his books is his favorite, he says, "It's like children, you can't pick," only to correct himself, "I guess with sixteen children there is bound to be at least one runt."

Phil, the author.

Phil is a courtly man, not tall but well built. Despite his macho bravura ("We males were traumatized by Hemingway; anyway, that's our excuse"), he can be fastidious, as evidenced by his perfect handwriting on thank-you notes. He has full lips and a quick smile and his eyes light up whenever something delights him, which is often, his pleased gaze followed by—there is no other word for it—a snort. Phil is the kind of retro guy who still calls waitresses "hon," a practice he defends: "Most of them like it, especially if they are old. Besides, they all call me 'hon' back."

One mild morning, sitting out on the deck, he asked our then teenaged daughter and her friend Claire Lawlor if during the previous evening in Edgartown they had any "shameful misdeeds to report," but first he wanted to find out if it was true that Claire was planning to be a doctor.

"But you look so young," he said. "Who would go to you?"

Claire does look young for her age: How else do you get voted "class cutest" in high school? Yet she is a serious student, capable of being dull on certain subjects that enthrall her, such as indium-promoted coupling reactions. As a potential healer, she has only two flaws: she might have to be nudged to put down the latest Harry Potter before paying full attention in an operating theater, and as a die-hard Red Sox fan she might need to be reminded that her antipathy to the Yankees should not extend to their fans when in need of medical attention.

Phil glanced hopefully toward the girls.

"About last night. Any fun you shouldn't have had?"

"No," said one.

"Just ice cream," said the other.

"Too bad," said Phil, staring gloomily at his bowl of soggy cereal. "I guess I'll have to go back to my soft foods diet."

Phil, the disappointed codger.

Phil and Leslie were often accompanied by their dog Sage, an English setter, and later by Sky after Sage died. Sage enjoyed the company of our standard poodle Porsha and was obedient in inverse proportion to our own dog's lack of couth.

One summer both dogs arrived having had setbacks during the winter. Sage's was psychological in nature. She had gone to Leslie's sister's Take Your Dog to Work Day. When prizes were given out for best behaved, lowest bark, cleanest coat, etc., in an obvious miscarriage of justice, Sage was overlooked—the only dog to be left out.

As for Porsha, that previous December she had swallowed a foreign object, a pair of gym shorts. We almost lost her, not to mention definitely losing the gym shorts. She became the Holiday Darling, such that medical staff and office assistants lined the corridors for her triumphant release on Christmas Eve. Her illness was complicated because she had Addison's disease, a failure of the adrenal glands common to her species, the same ailment that plagued President Kennedy. If anyone asked about her treatment, we always said it was the same as Kennedy's, a heavy course of steroids followed by photos of Marilyn Monroe.

Sage's cousin, Sky, inadvertently caused the worst confrontation of neighbor vs. neighbor during our entire time on the Point.

One afternoon, following the pond shoreline as it wound around the Point away from the ocean, Phil and Leslie and young Sky landed on a sandbar that, unbeknownst to the explorers, led them directly onto Mal Jones's property. A bad scene. We should have warned our guests.

Years before, in the summer of 2003, Mal Jones no longer belonged just to us, but instead he commanded the attention of the world press, this curious figure who used to have contra dances at dawn, an aging Pan with a weathered face and lithe frame who occupied a generous spread of some of the most glorious real estate on the planet, but who still raised his own chickens.

The confrontation between Mal Jones and dog owner Karin Magid had been building.

More than once Jones had found some of his animals slaughtered, and more than once he suspected that the dogs belonging to a neighbor had wandered away from their own property, a horse farm, through the woods and onto his. So when he found dog hair wedged in the splinters of the plywood chicken coop, he took action, paying $400 to have the evidence evaluated for its DNA, later requesting reimbursement from the court. It was the first time in forensic history that such evidence was used to convict a dog of a crime. The dog owner offered to replace the chickens by age and breed, but Mal Jones held out for fifty dollars per dead bird.

Fearful that Sky was about to devour his chickens, Mal was not pleased, kicking our friends off his land. Mal surmised that the so-called intruders came from our house, and a few hours later, he showed up unannounced (against all island etiquette unless you are issuing a hurricane eviction notice or bringing a jar of homemade beach plum jam) and he threatened to shoot any and all dogs if they ever came near his chickens again.

Phil Caputo looked Mal in the eye and assumed the ramrod don't-fuck-with-me posture of a soldier in combat, issuing the following edict in a voice that reached into the darkest tunnels of wartime fury: "You don't want to do that."

Phil, the warrior.

Leslie wrote this account in the log:

In conducting an experiment on the limits of cell phone reception on the Point, we approached a neighbor's house with our dog Sky and greeted several fowl. A woman, 50-ish and wearing a purple muumuu, came flying out of the house and issued her own greeting, which consisted of enthusiastic oaths about dogs, chickens, wildlife, and riparian rights. Shortly thereafter, a man appeared chez Katzenbach, saying, "You were lucky my wife found your dog and not me."

John wrote:

Chicken Man, a.k.a. Mal Jones, was fortunate—the "no harm, no fowl" incident was handled so well by one and all. Had Mal actually harmed a dog like Sky, I would have—well . . .

One time during the winter months, Phil sent us a letter about how Leslie probably saved his life:

For a solid month of these last three months, I could barely get out of bed and was beginning to think very dark thoughts, to effect of, What the hell am I doing here if I can't do anything? *Finally, I went with Leslie to a cardiologist in San Francisco and this guy worked medical miracles. I was discharged from the hospital on Saturday, and flew back to Arizona the same day. After sleeping for 12 hours, I woke up Sunday morning feeling my old self again—Phil fine again. Actually, it felt like a resurrection. I am now able to get to work on my new book, to hike, ride horses, and do everything I used to do. It's wonderful. I would like to think that coming through an experience like this I would gain some startling new insight into life, but I am afraid the only wisdom I have to impart is that the hoary cliché—if you don't have your health, you don't have anything—is true. Leslie was magnificent through all of it, selfless and caring and rock-solid. So another cliché—besides health, the most valuable possession a man can have is the love of a good woman. The WASP race does come through when the chips are down. If the situation had been reversed, instead of helping Leslie, I probably would have composed a tragic opera.*

Phil, the grateful spouse.

Phil usually left it up to Leslie to write in the logs, but once in a while he took pen to hand, such as in this 2006 entry:

Bombs fall on Beirut, missiles explode in Israel, jihadists blow up Shiites in Baghdad and vice versa, but here at the Point, all things are possible in this best of all possible places. Anyhow, here there's no such thing as too much of a good thing.

Phil, the philosopher.

After dinner we often retired to the deck and, wrapped in sweaters and blankets, we admired the stars, a clear dusting against a dark dome if we were lucky, and we would talk, or rather, we would talk just enough to get Phil, a born storyteller, to take over. He often talked about the early days of working at newspapers.

Some of his stories were a sort of anti-lullaby, better for daylight, like the one about the time he was imprisoned in Beirut, or when he died in Africa (only to be revived in some kind of elaborate miracle that may or may not have the ring of truth), or when he had to clear brush with a machete from the runway of a primitive airport before being able to take off and thus avoid armed pursuers. He always recited his story about covering a crime story from the fire escape on the eighteenth floor of a hotel in Chicago word for word, using the same pauses, same harrumphs, same wise nods of the head.

"It must have been 1968 or 1969. I was working at the *Trib* in Chicago and a group of young Japanese tourists had come to town and two of them, two girls, were raped and murdered on the eighteenth floor of one of the most posh hotels in Chicago at the time.

"Well, this was, as you can imagine, raw meat for all the general assignment and police reporters. Mayor Daley assigned four Chicago policemen to guard the hotel corridor, four Chicago cops who could have been defensive linemen for the Chicago Bears. There was no getting through them. Now this was the old get-me-rewrite days of journalism, and when I called my city editor, Don Agrella, he wanted something exclusive. I told him these guys were a wall of muscle and a wall of silence and all we had were the bare facts, so he suggested I get a description of the crime scene. Don suggested I go out on the fire escape and walk on the catwalk to room number, oh, 1805, let's say, and I was young, twenty-six years old, so I said, *Sure, why not?* even though I was really afraid of heights, and I found myself eighteen floors above the Loop with my back glued to the brick wall trying to control my utter terror. I inched my way down with my eyes glancing inside all the hotel's windows when I finally came to the room and the curtains were open, and I could look inside and see one of the girls draped over a bathtub and there's a curtain that had been torn down, maybe she was trying to grab it, and blood, a lot of blood splashed all over. I slowly inched my way back into the hotel and called Don up and gave him this description. I probably got a little florid. I might have even imagined a detail or two for all I know, and after I hung up I noticed this young reporter from the *Chicago Daily News* had been listening in. Now he was from a p.m. paper and the *Chicago Tribune* was a morning paper, but I knew his lock-up for that day's copy and ours were about the same time. So of course he's gotta get what we got, and I saw him head on out and the minute he did I went up to the fire door, which had this big brass handle that locked from the inside. You could unlock it if you needed to get out in an emergency, but otherwise no one could get in, so I pulled the bar up and not much later I heard this tug on the door, and then this banging and pounding, and I waited and waited until

I was sure his paper was past lock-up and then I opened the door and I let him back in."

Phil, the fierce competitor.

Phil grew up in the suburbs of Chicago in a traditional Italian household with one sister, two years younger, whose job it was to make his bed every day. He learned how to make his own bed in the military: "I realized as a recruit during boot camp I couldn't really turn to the drill sergeant and demand, 'Where's my sister?'" After getting this information, I was tempted to contact the U.S. Marine Corps personally, thanking them for taking Phil in, where, at the very least, he learned how to manage his own linens.

We were always elated whenever Phil volunteered to prepare his grandmother's stuffed swordfish *rollatini* in marinara sauce. He asked Sandy (at John's Fish Market) to cut the steaks in half so that they then could be pounded, stuffed, and tied before being browned on the grill and then baked in the oven, smothered in a homemade marinara sauce. When I heard that she had asked Phil for his recipe, I felt, I confess, a stab of jealousy.

Phil is one of those noisy, theatrical cooks who would have it no other way. For this one dish, he used the top of the stove, the oven, and the outdoor grill at various critical stages of the daylong enterprise. He required a slew of sous chefs, preferably Justine and her pals Claire and Jen when they were in their mid- to late teens, to dice, mince, pound, knead, and stir a variety of ingredients. "They are more attentive than the boys," he said. "Plus, I like to think of them as vestal virgins, with the hope that the second of those two words is accurate."

When all was said and done, about the only kitchen operation he appeared to avoid was poaching. Well, also cleanup.

In addition to preparing seafood and telling stories, Phil's other suit as a guest was that he was available to fish, fishing being a more delicate subject than one might think, due to what can only be called a Bible-sized spate of bad luck that has lasted for years.

The logs often featured the same weary yet frequent notation.

Fish: None in the sea but plenty in the fish store.

We watched John and Phil getting ready, hope flooding their faces.

We saw all the commotion: the waders and the vests, the poles and the flies.

We observed, as John's verbally efficient sister Anne once put it, "much rubber worn."

Yet, time after time, they return home empty-handed.

We have a map of the island, created by a guest named Al Larkin, marked with Xs, denoting the places where no fish had ever been caught, in effect blotting out the entire shoreline.

If you pin John and Phil down, they will explain the reasons fishing can be less than successful. They name outside forces beyond their control. They will tell you about how the worst time to fish on the Vineyard is in August, because that is when the fish flee for colder waters. They talk about how dinner parties scheduled during a rising tide with a full moon are a waste of a rising tide and a full moon. They talk about calibrations in water temperature and the cruel, conniving nature of a bad wind. They get misty-eyed as they audition their flies, wondering which would work best: the Lefty's Deceivers or the clouser minnows and perhaps surf candy. Blue and white? Red and white? All white?

The one time they caught a twenty-pound striped bass keeper, Phil and John arrived back at the house at close to midnight. Everyone was ready to hit the sack except them, with Phil prepping the fish on the deck and John firing up the grill. I was sated and sleepy but did my best to inquire, with as much enthusiasm as I could muster, if I could perhaps have a small bite, knowing the answer could only be yes.

Phil, the fisherman, kind of, sort of, maybe.

A few years back, the *Associated Press* ran a story with the headline "Fly Fishing Gets Women's Touch," which became the subject of that night's dinner conversation. The article quoted president of the American Fly Fishers Trade Association:

"Fly fishing has this stigma of being a cigar-smoking, good-old-boys-type club. It would be great to change that image."

Phil: "What did the story say? Women like fly-fishing. Well, why not? I'm not surprised. I've known about this for years." Pause. "Fly-fishing is perfect for women."

Perfect, Phil? How so?

He started to say fly-fishing is perfect for women because they can do it in bare feet.

"Have you," we asked him, "heard of Betty Friedan and Gloria Steinem?"

"The Equal Rights Amendment?"

"Or seen *Thelma and Louise*?"

Pausing ever so slightly, waving his hand to dismiss any previous remarks, he took it from the top:

"Really, fly-fishing is a sport that requires precision, attention to detail, and patience. Men get so macho about it. They throw the line too hard as if the skill is strength, not motion. Men think it's like slamming a tennis racket."

We all then enjoyed the dinner Phil had prepared with:

Admirable precision.

Scrupulous attention to detail.

Lots of patience.

And a ton of garlic.

Phil, the kitchen god.

Chapter Eleven

What Kay Graham Brought to the Table

During the summer from 1989 until her death in 2001, we had an annual rendezvous with Katharine Graham, the publisher of the *Washington Post* who in July and August was also the doyenne of Martha's Vineyard, slim in her summer slacks, words spoken with a touch of well-bred lockjaw, presiding over events at her magnificent property called Mohu.

Shortly after arriving on the island, my husband and I would receive a letter on expensive thick blue paper, signed by Liz Hylton, Mrs. Graham's personal assistant:

> *Dear Maddy and John,*
> *I am beginning to feel like your pen pal.*

TO THE NEW OWNERS

Mrs. Graham asks if she might tempt you to come to lunch on Saturday or Sunday (if you have someone with whom you can leave your children). It would be you and your houseguests, Mrs. Graham, Henry Kissinger (and Nancy K. if she can come at the last minute), Senator William Cohen of Maine, and (national security adviser Lieutenant General) Brent Scowcroft. One o'clock whichever day works best for you.

The document would be hand-delivered by a member of Mrs. Graham's staff, who drove the dirt road, up and back. At that time, the house had no phone, and we all took pride in the faux ruggedness of corresponding in such an old-fashioned, Jane Austen way.

My favorite part of the letter will always be the parenthetical aside: *if you have someone with whom you can leave your children.* The notion of taking our children at that time in their lives to such a gathering gave rise to awkward scenarios: my son discussing firecrackers and his latest soccer cleats with Kissinger or my daughter insisting on everyone doing the hokey-pokey.

We sent our regrets and found another time to see each other.

I have never been certain what "Mohu" stands for. Perhaps Mohu is an old Wampanoag term for something earthbound and nature-worshipping, involving still skies and seagulls and salt air, though it could also have had a secondary meaning along the lines of "a really excellent real estate investment." The story goes that Mrs. Graham purchased the 218-acre estate in Lambert's Cove in 1972 at the behest of newspaper editor Henry Beetle Hough, who wanted to keep the property out of the hands of developers. The house—with views of the water, furniture covered in white, and round tables for dining that seated up to ten guests—felt like the set of a Katharine Hepburn movie, one in which the heroine shows verbal spunk and athletic grace in equal measure. At the entrance was a stack of straw hats for guests to borrow as a shield against the sun in the event that lunch or drinks were on the patio. Mrs. Graham's way of receiving company was reminiscent of a long-ago time that was very elegant and is very gone. She stood at five feet nine inches tall, a height that underscored her natural grace. Before dinner she served simple drinks and hors d'oeuvres in the French style, kept to a discrete minimum, never anything showy or loudly caloric, no Bahama Mamas and no vat of guacamole and sour cream with a jolly name like "piranha dip." If you arrived at Mohu before everyone else, you might be treated to a gabfest about the upcoming guests: who was overrated, who was sleeping with whom, who was a drama queen ("She can turn the simple act of boiling an egg into a three-act play"), and who was the real deal, possessing true talent that never dims. Punctuality paid off.

Our first invitation from Mrs. Graham was verbal and off-hand, issued at a memorial service in June 1989 for a former *Washington Post* editor, Howard Simons.

Simons was an underrated player in the Watergate saga. He had been working as night editor on a desultory Friday to Saturday overnight shift on June 17, 1972, in the nation's capital when two disconnected, seemingly comic events attracted Simons's attention: the robbery at the Watergate of the Democratic National Committee Headquarters by five men wearing surgical gloves, including one who said he worked for the CIA, who were arrested at 2:30 a.m., and a car crash into someone's house while two people were making love on a sofa. The next day, Simons reported to Mrs. Graham, and at the time they both chuckled, having no reason to disagree with Ron Ziegler, President Nixon's press secretary, who dismissed the robbery as a "third-rate burglary attempt," warning that "certain elements may try to stretch this beyond what it is."

Later, Mrs. Graham wrote, "None of us, of course, had any idea how far the story would stretch; the beginning—once the laughter died down—all seemed so farcical."

I was taken aback by her request ("You must call when you get to the island and we will find a time to get together") but felt an obligation to honor it. None of us ever feels as if we know all the rules to a good life, but surely one is that if someone you admire on the scale that I admired Mrs. Graham says you must call, you do. As a publisher, Mrs. Graham had gone mano a mano with the Nixon White House and had subjected herself to threats and ridicule, including bizarre comments from the then attorney general John Mitchell, who said, "Katie Graham's gonna get her tit caught in a big fat wringer."

For many of the years that we knew her, we witnessed a decline in her physical capabilities, mostly due to a bad hip that halted her gait and eroded her usually spirited game of tennis. Eventually, hip replacement gave her a new lease.

We knew she was working on her memoir and it seemed to be taking an uncomfortably long time to complete. When *Personal History* finally appeared in 1997, to the tune of 625 pages long, I remember feeling relieved—relieved that it was done and also relieved, after I read it, that it was written in the style of the best memoirs, with no regard to inflating the author's virtues and with all due diligence in recording the more vulnerable moments. In college, depressed, she confessed to wearing the same sweater every day for a year.

Personal History has an air of detached dignity, as if the author is beyond currying favor or proving points. She sacrifices the latest gossip for the long view. Her audience appears not to be her children or even her grandchildren, but descendants yet to be born, who might want to know what it was like when their great-great-great-grandmother was running the world.

Mrs. Graham combined power in public space with vulnerability in the private sector. She inherited the helm at the *Post* from her handsome, charismatic husband who drank, was verbally abusive, went on buying binges, and at one point threatened to run off with his mistress, taking his majority share in the Washington Post Company with him. He shot himself in the head at their country house.

A longtime fan of memoirs, I have often pondered the difference between them and autobiography. In the end, to my way of thinking, autobiographies tend to encompass the full span of a life and are usually written by people who occupy some kind of public space: ex-presidents, ambassadors, heads of the Federal Reserve. Memoirs are written by less obviously eminent sorts. Generals write autobiographies; foot soldiers write memoirs. *Personal History* is unusual in that it is both an autobiography and a memoir because its author is both a general and a foot soldier. Mrs. Graham was at the center of history as a major publisher, often referred to in her heyday as the most powerful woman in the world, and also at its outskirts: a single woman bringing up four children on her own.

Having had the job of publisher thrust upon her, she writes: "I had very little idea of what I was supposed to be doing, so I set out to learn. What I essentially did was to put one foot in front of the other, shut my eyes, and step off the edge."

In her book she said that one of the biggest regrets of her life occurred on the day after her husband's funeral, when, in a daze, she continued with a plan to sail on a yacht in Istanbul that had been chartered by her mother, traveling to Europe with her daughter, Lally, and sending two of her sons, Bill and Steve, back to camp and her son Don back to his summer job.

> That decision may have been right for me, but it was so wrong for Bill and Steve and even for Don—so wrong that I wonder how I could have made it. Would my younger boys have been better off going too? Would it have been better if I'd stayed home for them? This is, for me, the most painful thing to look back on. It's hard to remake decisions and even harder to rethink nondecisions. Sometimes you don't really decide, you just move forward, and that is what I did—moved forward blindly and mindlessly into a new and unknown life.

As for taking over the *Post*, she always underplayed what it must have been like to walk that gangplank: "The surprise was that I landed on my feet."

And so once a summer, when we saw each other, alternating houses, it was always a thrill but also unnerving. I would always fret about what to serve. She would have been chagrinned to learn that I felt so . . . discombobulated. In her manner she conveyed the fiction that we were on an even playing field, hostess-wise, which would have been true if only I had my own full-time French chef, gifts of dish sets from world leaders, and guests who ran countries on a routine basis. One time I served grilled swordfish from John's

Fish Market, assured by Sandy that it had been harpooned rather than long-lined. That way, the fish comes out of the water alive, which makes the meat fresher and firmer. This environmentally sound way of catching the fish jacks up the flavor but inflates the price. My sole culinary intrusion was to gussy it up with the sheerest membrane of store-bought mayonnaise to seal in the flavor before putting it on the grill. I am a minimalist when it comes to local food.

When Mrs. Graham insisted that I share my recipe with her chef, I was so embarrassed that I had not concocted some kind of fancy rémoulade that I pretended to be one of those secret-hoarding cooks, and I said I would be happy to exchange the information for, oh, say, the identity of Deep Throat.

"My dear," she said in her low, cultured voice, "you drive a hard bargain."

The next time we served her lobster, the delicacy for which today's diners nearly abase themselves, but which was so plentiful in the nineteenth century that the Commonwealth of Massachusetts, as an act of humane legislation, passed a bill forbidding the feeding of lobster to prison inmates, at least not for all three meals a day. The theory behind serving lobster to Mrs. Graham was that it automatically makes hierarchies vanish, what with the infantilizing bibs and the projectile juices and the debate over whether the yucky parts are edible, not to mention the sound effects: the pounding, the cracking, the slurps, the satisfied sighs.

That night we talked about life in Washington.

As a guest, Nancy Doherty, wrote afterward, "We learned some interesting facts. She voted for George Bush the first, Bobby Kennedy once reduced her to tears, she thinks Teddy needs to clean up his act big-time, and she eats lobster with admirable gusto . . . in short, she is one of the most impressive icons we've ever spent an evening with."

I always felt stumped when it came to hostess gifts for Mrs. Graham. The usual bottle of wine or tea towels or soap seemed all wrong, especially considering the competition, such as when her brother-in-law Senator Bob Graham visited from Florida, bringing not only avocados and key limes from the Sunshine State, but also the news that he might run for national office.

In certain circles, I deduced, the ultimate hostess gift is Presidential Buzz.

When I praised the colorfully painted plates on which dinner was served, she said, "Those were from the king of Jordan. He visited here and afterward sent a huge crate of dishes."

Another pricey-looking keepsake: "Oh, I have Princess Di to thank for that. What a lovely young woman."

My offerings were more humble.

When water shoes first came out, I gave her a pair (she seemed delighted), and on another occasion I brought her a stack of memoirs, including my two standbys, *This Boy's Life* by Tobias Wolff and *A Moveable Feast* by Ernest Hemingway, because I thought reading them might help her with her own memoir. Unlike writers working in other genres, who often shy away from reading the competition lest they borrow its rhythms or fall prey to disabling feelings of inferiority about their own work in comparison, memoir writers usually read far and wide in the field, with a cunning eye not only for content, but also in order to have an interior conversation about what they have read in order to explore how one's own life compares with the one being described.

In the 1990s, when the Clintons started showing up on the Vineyard with increasing frequency, Mrs. Graham was constantly asked whether she would be entertaining them. Her response never varied. It was airy and self-protective: "I have no plans at the moment. I take my orders from Vernon"—Vernon being Vernon Jordan, Bill Clinton's confidant and golfing buddy. (Jordan and his wife had a custom of going to Mrs. Graham's for dinner on their first night on the island every summer, no matter how late, as a way of sounding a certain gong.) She found it amusing that the very people who were the first to decry the "dreadful commotion" a presidential visit inevitably stirs were also the ones to lobby most boldly for an invitation to her dinners in his honor.

John's parents were among the invitees. Thanks to Lydia, we have in the log a diagram of the seating arrangement at one such gathering and this 1993 account:

> *We've had delightful visits and fun with the Clintons at Kay Graham's, Jackie Onassis at her beach, and old friends at our house and around the island. As Maddy likes the details, here are a few on the dinner with the President and Mrs. Clinton. Both Nick and I enjoyed both Clintons. We came away from dinner especially impressed with HRC, feeling with her intelligence, wit, and warmth she could easily be president herself. Maybe she will be.*

The topics we covered at Mrs. Graham's non-presidential dinners included the ardor of traveling by steamship to the island. Ron Rappaport, the attorney then representing the Steamship

Authority, defended a recent wave of cancellations of the ferry due to bad weather.

Mrs. Graham looked up, puzzled: "Ron! If you can't reverse an act of God, what kind of lawyer are you?"

In some ways all this clever talk and good food were just a cover, because there was something else about Mrs. Graham that made these yearly visits stand out, and it was her obvious desire to connect in part because my husband and I were the same age as her children, more or less, three of whom we met at her house over the years, and our children were the same ages as her grandchildren. I feel the invitations emanated from an admirable impulse to mix it up, to go beyond one's own age group.

In the end, my debt of gratitude to her extended beyond our summertime socializing. At one point when I was struggling over whether I should write about the family I grew up in, Mrs. Graham was supportive. I explained that my mother had been widowed and her life was led in the shadow of the future she never had.

"Your mother raised six children on her own?"

She paused, lowering her eyelids as if to look as much inward as outward.

She spoke softly.

"Believe me. That's a story."

The last time I saw Mrs. Graham was at a reading at Politics & Prose in Washington. The bookstore owners were eager that she be seated in a comfortable chair, but she acted embarrassed, as the last thing she wanted to do was appear enthroned. Afterward, she joined me and my sister Jacqueline (reporting for *USA Today*), *Washington Times* editor Hank Pearson, *Post* veteran Athelia Knight, and others at a restaurant that we chose for its close location so as to minimize the amount of walking Mrs. Graham would have to do. Her pace was slow, but she resisted being led by the elbow. I remember glancing down at the sidewalk and noticing her shoes, sleek pumps pretty enough to verge on the impractical. What I liked about her shoes was their defiance: an emblem in honor of the glad girl she must once have been. The restaurant proved too loud and the dinner passed too quickly, and when I walked Mrs. Graham out to her car and to the driver who awaited her, we vowed to see each other soon, in early August, on the Vineyard. A few weeks later, in July 2001, she fell down and lost consciousness at a business meeting out in Sun Valley, Idaho. She died several days later.

From the obituary in the *Gazette*:

Mrs. Graham was a benefactor—both noisy and quiet—to many worthy causes on the Vineyard. At the annual Possible Dreams Auction for Martha's Vineyard Community Services she peddled herself, along with lunches and tours of the *Washington Post*, and helped to raise tens of thousands of dollars over the years. In 1997 she was the top "dream," bringing in $100,000 when three people bid against each other for the prize. Mrs. Graham satisfied all three bidders by agreeing to host three separate lunches and matching their $25,000 bids with one of her own.

Lunch with Katharine Graham was again listed as a possible dream in the program for this year's auction, set for early August.

She also quietly gave money to many other nonprofit groups on the Vineyard.

She never tried to cross swords with town government on the Vineyard. When she proposed building a pier on her property 10 years ago, and it quickly became apparent that the pier plan was at odds with many environmental interests, she withdrew the application.

"She always avoided confrontation with the town if she could. I think she was perhaps one of the most dignified people who lived on the Island," said West Tisbury selectman John Alley, who knew Mrs. Graham for 30 years, both as a town official and as a friend.

"About once a year she called me—sometimes it was to ask something about the Vineyard or something about her property, and sometimes it was just to say hello," Mr. Alley said.

He said Mrs. Graham always told him to go to Mohu in the fall and harvest her grapes—and he often did. One year he made grape jelly and during a trip to the capital he left a jar for her at the *Washington Post*.

"I think the town of West Tisbury and the Island will miss Kay Graham and this certainly is the end of an era. I was shocked to hear the news," Mr. Alley said.

Her funeral at Washington National Cathedral attracted thousands.

Bach was played.

Bells tolled.

The Twenty-Third Psalm was read.

Anthems were sung, including "America the Beautiful."

More music:

Respighi.

Handel.

Former executive editor of the *Post* Ben Bradlee said his one-time boss was a "spectacular dame," adding: "What a way to go! Lunch with Tom Hanks and Rita Wilson on that last day. Bridge with Warren Buffett and Bill Gates the day before. Dinner the night before that, with admiring moguls galore, plus the new president of Mexico. And now Yo-Yo Ma, to send you on your storied way.

"Not bad for the widowed mother of four, who started her career at the top, thirty-eight years ago, in great tragedy and great trepidation . . .

"Speaking of 'widowed mother of four,' did you ever hear of the 'Widowed Grandmother Defense,' developed by our lawyers when Spiro T. Agnew tried to subpoena our reporters' notes in a last-ditch effort to escape jail?

"We had refused to surrender those notes. Reporters don't own their own notes, Joe Califano told the district court. The owner of the paper owns them. And let's see if they dare throw Katharine Graham in jail.

"She was delighted at the prospect. Maybe not all of you understand exactly what it takes to make a great newspaper. It takes a great owner. Period. An owner who committed herself with passion and the highest standards in principles to a simple search for truth. With fervor, not favor. With fairness and courage . . .

"This is what Kay Graham brought to the table, plus so much more."

Katharine Graham belonged to the world. She belonged to the *Washington Post*, to Ben Bradlee and to his wife, journalist Sally Quinn, to fancy talk at fancy dinner parties.

Yet the times I remember Mrs. Graham as most tickled had little to do with noisy commercial enterprise or with witty repartee or with history in the making, but rather when she anticipated a visit from her children and especially her then young grandchildren, discussing when they would be on the island and what they might like to do. The menu would take a sudden casual turn. A cookout. Peanut butter. Chocolate milk.

She loved to tell the story about how she learned she had won the Pulitzer for *Personal History* from her son Don, who took over as publisher of the *Post* after she retired. She had been out of town for the day. The weather was tumultuous and a scary bumpy flight is a scary bumpy flight no matter how much of a globetrotter you are. She was still shaky when she got home. Don was there to greet her, with a big grin and the words that made it all worthwhile:

"We did it."

She would repeat the first word, "We," pleased with the plural, with its implication not just for herself, but also her family; its honor in the face of tragedy.

On another occasion she sounded giddy when she recounted a toast one of her other children gave her at what I believe was her eightieth birthday party. She was pleased by something Steve, her youngest, said, and I can only paraphrase her paraphrase, something I must make clear since hers is a family of journalists, and I do not want to appear to be transcribing when I am not.

I know you think it was terrible to take off like you did for Turkey after our father's death and that you felt it was important to tell everyone who read your book how bad you felt, but I want you to know I forgive you. I forgive you for a lot of other things, like how I never had a pony or the time the driver was late picking me up at boarding school. But there is one thing I cannot forgive. I liked it when you got me and my friends tickets to the Rolling Stones. That was cool. And they were really good seats. There was only one problem. Did you really have to sit with us?

Of course.

She was a *mom.*

How could she resist?

I have often thought of her since her death in the summer right before 9/11 and wondered how she would have interpreted the years that have followed. What would she have made of George Bush the second, whose social pedigree would have hit the right notes for her but whose odd, flawed tenure as president would surely have dismayed her? Would she have been proud of Hillary Clinton for surviving marital humiliation on a gargantuan scale, reincarnating herself as the first woman to run for president as the nominee of a major political party? Would she have warmed to Barack Obama who, like Clinton, chose Martha's Vineyard as his vacation spot? How would she have reacted if she were alive in October 2013 and witnessed the sale of the *Washington Post* to Amazon's Jeff Bezos? Did she have even an inkling of the extent to which technological advances would revamp what constitutes news and its delivery systems, of the ways in which once mighty newspapers would morph and downsize and disappear, of how her own beloved *Post* would first be rebranded as a media company, then kept afloat for a time thanks to the purchase of Kaplan, the company hell-bent on stumping high school students taking their SATS with words like "eschew" and "fulsome" and "gloaming," and then, in what may be the final moment of infamy, purchased in a fire sale by Bezos, the *Post's* headquarters in Washington now torn down. As for her opinion of Donald Trump . . .

Mrs. Graham's eight-thousand-square-foot summerhouse built in the 1920s, Mohu, is now gone. Her son Bill loved the spot it was on, but felt it was a white elephant, dominating a magnificent setting. He contacted a Vineyard-based ecologically minded salvage company, South Mountain Company, and hired its workers to "undevelop it"—a process described on its website:

> He [Bill] wanted to know if we could cut it up and move it and make affordable housing out of it. It was way at the end of a long narrow dirt road flanked by stone walls. It wasn't feasible to move it without cutting it into tiny pieces. But it was an incredibly evocative house, rich with fine materials.
>
> "How about this?" we asked him. "Why don't you pay us to dismantle it piece by piece? We can save 90% of the material and you can donate it to the Island Affordable Housing Fund and we'll use it to build affordable housing." He agreed enthusiastically. Undevelopment. Now that's a concept, isn't it?
>
> For three months 12 people worked in that house day in and day out. About 50,000 BF of fine lumber was salvaged, along with assorted other fine materials. At the end two stone chimneys were left standing in a magnificent restored landscape of native grasses.
>
> It's not always possible to deconstruct buildings slated for demolition. Some just don't lend themselves to it; more often owners don't want to take the time or pay the money (it's very labor intensive). But it's disturbing

to see the wealth of valuable materials that find their way into the landfills. We are always working on new ways to save more and more of the treasure that now goes to waste.

The materials salvaged from Mohu included vertical grain Douglas fir flooring, quarry tiles, and yellow pine beadboard. Now the bluff sits empty—save for the two tall chimneys.

Chapter Twelve
Boiling the Pope

Yes, I was intimidated by Lydia King Phelps Stokes Katzenbach.

Before I met her, I had a vague expectation that Lydia would be like other Protestant women of means, a familiar type, upbeat but reserved. I assumed she would be given to using the word "marvelous" (dropping the r in favor of h) to describe everything from a spectacular sunset to a full tank of gas. In her appearance and her style, I imagined Talbots and tweed, a subdued couture consisting of rose-colored cardigans and denim wraparound skirts.

She surprised me, not just her dramatic updo, but the whole package. Her demeanor ranged from regal to renegade. For work, she preferred suits made by tailors in Tokyo. The jackets draped perfectly. The skirts ended right below the knee. The blouses were soft and feminine. For dress-up, she favored a more sweeping look. Her favorite designer was Koos van den Akker, whose work often featured rich fabrics with contrasting prints and seams made of ribbons. At one of our first meetings, she leaned over and said, sotto voce, "Missoni is *your* designer." With that quick phrase, I was ushered into the world of fancy salons and private fittings—knighted. I was ushered out just as quickly when she said, "Of course you'll have to learn how to use makeup." (A classic example of the push-pull inherent in the mother-in-law, daughter-in-law equation.)

Lydia cited ancestors who were the subjects of paintings by Turner in the National Gallery the way someone else might reference how an aunt's famous marshmallow Jell-O salad was always a big hit at the company picnic. When she was six she was provided with the same doll as Queen Elizabeth because, well, because of course. When she was twenty-one she was given a pearl ring surrounded by diamonds. Her dining room table featured silver ice buckets and tiny tongs just for olives.

Like FDR, she couldn't wait to be a traitor to her class, to break out of her inherited caste system and to find her way into a more fluid society. She aspired to a certain bohemian outrageousness and never stopped beaming from an early school report: "Lydia is a born leader, but in the wrong direction."

Her childhood summers were spent in the heart of old white male privilege in the Adirondacks. In *Camp Chronicles* by Mildred Phelps Stokes Hooker, published in 1964, the author described how the Stokes family would travel early in the twentieth century to the island by train, by wagon (about forty miles), and by boat, in a party of ten family members, with an equal number of servants, as well as "three horses, two dogs, one carriage, five large boxes of tents, three cases of wine, two packages of stovepipe, two stoves, one bale china, one iron pot, four washstands, one barrel of hardware, four bundles of poles, seventeen cots and seventeen mattresses, four canvas packages, one buckboard," not to mention twenty-five trunks, thirteen small boxes, and one boat.

An ad from 1914 in *Country Life in America* gives a sense of its grandeur:

> Containing one large cabin with sitting-room, dining-room, pantry, kitchen and servants' hall. One cabin with 2 bedrooms and bath; two smaller cabins with dressing-rooms and detached bath and toilet; one tent; one servants' house with 4 bedrooms; one guide house with 2 bedrooms. One boathouse with boudoir or bedroom above; one launch house.
>
> The entire camp has been done over since last occupied; is completely furnished, including bed and table linen, plated ware, etc. Will be rented for 3 months from June 15th for $2,000, or from June 1st to October 1st for $2,500, including use of 1 canoe, 1 sailboat and 2 rowboats. Also all wood and ice.

We visited John's cousin Phelps in the Adirondacks in the summer of 1989 for a week. I was curious about how this dark green place with tall trees had become a symbol of so much that was stifling and oppressive for Lydia. Surely her preference for the Vineyard had more to it than simply black flies vs. ticks.

The camp was decorated with bearskin rugs, furniture crafted from twigs, and the stuffed heads of deer and moose and other vanquished prey. One night I had the choice of sitting in the living room avoiding the glass eyes of dead animals or participating in the old Protestant custom of Sunday Evening Sing. I chose the latter and rode in a motorboat to the home of some neighbors, where we sang "Faith of Our Fathers," and songs like it, with thin rhymes and low-key sentiments, for about an hour. These songs seemed to be aimed at a blue-chip sort of deity, one who had likely gone to business school and favored rep ties. When the singing finished, talk turned to tie-up-the-harbor parties, boat races, upcoming doubles, and the weather, accompanied by a wan assortment of sugar cookies and orange juice. Someone explained that the boats for the races were Idems, thirteen of which were built especially for the wind conditions on Upper Saint Regis Lake. All are still in use except the one in a museum. For Lydia, the Adirondacks had an inbred quality: similar people with similar views and similar backgrounds. She wanted a larger, less claustrophobic, less rule-ridden world. We came to it from different directions, but this was one of our most powerful meeting places.

She found the anti-Semitism on the lake mystifying and hor-rifying. Her parents' best friends were Simeon Strunsky, the first to write the Topics of the Times column in the *New York Times*, and his wife, Manya Gordon, an advocate for the labor unions (a possible Communist!).

"When they visited us on a summer holiday at Pearl Island, my parents could not/would not take them with them to any social/family gatherings on the lake 'so as not to embarrass them as they were Jewish.' All very, very confusing for a child to understand, as I thought the Strunskys were, especially Simeon Strunsky, the warmest, funniest, and friendliest and most interesting friends my parents had."

Lydia remembered going to an Upper Saint Regis Property Owners' Association meeting and hearing a cousin offer a vote of thanks to neighbors who had resisted selling their camp to Jews.

During the years when Nick was in Washington, Lydia was a popular hostess. On one occasion thirteen-year-old John and his best friend, Craig McNamara (of Beetlebung Corner fame, and son of Robert, documented earlier), arrived home in the late afternoon after a day spent outdoors playing the Kennedy-inspired D.C. sport of touch football. Like any kids that age, they went immediately to the refrigerator. There, inside, they spotted a platter of twelve of what Craig instantly dubbed "mini-steaks" wrapped delicately in bacon. It did not take more than seconds for John to find a frying pan—and the two boys instantly set to (a) frying the mini-steaks and (b) devouring them. Craig often remarked: "Well, why wouldn't you fry those mini-steaks? They fit in the pan perfectly."

John's version:

"Eight had disappeared in this manner when my mother entered the kitchen and saw, to her horror, the filet mignon prepped for that night's dinner featuring Princess Margaret and Lord Snowdon of British royalty, alongside Craig's secretary of defense dad and mother Marg, erased from the menu. This, naturally, was in the days when grocery stores actually closed for the evening at six P.M. She frantically dialed the number for the nearest Giant Food and was connected to the butcher."

"Sorry, ma'am. We're closing right now."

Pause. Icy voice.

"No, you are not."

As usual, Lydia got her way.

Replacement filets were acquired—the butcher standing outside the store waiting for Lydia to arrive, the carefully bacon-wrapped meat in his hands. The bill got paid a few days later. (It was, as noted, a *far* different time.) British and Washington royalty were well fed. International diplomatic crisis averted. John and Craig escaped unharmed.

Lydia was such a sought-after hostess that she scored the ultimate coup of serving as a punch line in a Herblock cartoon in which a woman scolds her husband, "How can I do the Monkey at Lydia's when I am married to a baboon of a husband?" *Look* magazine ran a picture of her sitting sidesaddle on one of the family's two antique carved carousel animals, a donkey named Bianca, poised for eternity in the rampant position. She was a beauty, with a lush face and generous features, especially big eyes and high cheekbones. Papers in the South used to run her photo with the skin tinted darker, claiming that the only reason her husband fought for civil rights was because his wife was a Negro. She responded by helping to found an organization that promoted the admission of minority students to private schools.

When the Democrats left office in 1968, the Katzenbachs moved north. Shortly after, they bought the property on the Vineyard, perhaps as a way to soften the blow for John's father from going from the epicenter of global power to the more routine life as a corporate lawyer at IBM, commuting from Riverdale to the town we used to jokingly call "Honk Honk Armonk," working for over a dozen years on an antitrust case brought by the government against the company.

At the same time Lydia embarked on training for her career as a psychoanalyst, having been led to do so because of her own analysis. Lydia said her mother was not tuned in to the needs of small children, proven by her oft-repeated conviction, "Children under the age of five are just rabbits." The factors that brought Lydia to the couch belong to her, but after that experience she flourished, eager to act on her belief in the uniqueness of everyone's personal story. One time, she had a studio built for her practice, and she chose to install a variety of windows, not one the same size or dimension. I know that she helped many people. Former patients kept in touch. One gave her a handmade quilt, which adorned a bed on the Vineyard. Another sent Lydia her first novel while it was still hot off the presses. The author was then in her late sixties, and it was long after treatment had ended. At a book award ceremony given by the National Alliance on Mental Illness, a prize recipient told me how much he owed to her, as a person and as a writer.

She once told me about a patient whose daughter had returned from a semester abroad ravaged by drugs. The patient and her husband were about to put their entire life on hold when Lydia cautioned them not to, sharing the content of a letter she sent to them, but leaving out any identifying details.

The more you cancel your life, the more you are communicating to the child, "You're so fragile. Look at what you have done to our lives." And that is only going to make your daughter feel more vulnerable and chaotic than she already does. The more you can keep your own life going as usual the more she can hope to feel stable within herself and not further crippled by how disabled you have also become. You have to show her the path to separateness, stability, and life-ongoing. With that in mind, every time you look at her, every time you stand in front of her, speak to her, listen to her, laugh with her, get angry or worried about her when she is in your presence, you have to see her and the person you know her to be: gifted, intelligent, creative, empathic, sane, humorous, delightful, embraceable, and a success. That is the only way she will be able to reflect her view of herself. No matter what the reality, you have to reflect those known positives all the time. If not, you will all be caught in the trap of seeing only the symptoms of your fears and that will be her only reflection of herself.

Lydia's favorite saying other than "Never write the ending": "Reality is overrated."

In 1985 when Marg McNamara died, Lydia gave the eulogy at the National Cathedral. Several years later, in a reception line at the first Bush White House, both George H. W. Bush and his wife, Barbara, gave Nick and Lydia firm bipartisan handshakes and then, looking straight at Nick, said they would never forget the beautiful speech he gave on behalf of Marg McNamara. They misremembered the event in the apparent belief that powerful words must have emanated from a powerful man, not his spouse.

It was a telling moment for Lydia and one that encapsulated the feeling she had had about Washington for a long time: it has a way of making people feel invisible, especially women, regardless of their husband's status.

In her work Lydia addressed the secret gears and inner workings of each patient—the opposite of Washington.

She celebrated what is invisible.

Born with a sense of design, she could make any interior within her range of influence a place of refuge and beauty. Her husband admired her photographic memory for color. One time she pointed out to me with pride that the exterior of a new Jeep blended perfectly with the landscape on the island. It bothered her that her grandchildren's Fisher-Price toys were in bright unambiguous primary colors: Who decided that children would not like blocks in chartreuse and magenta and persimmon? She winced when the seam of a lampshade was exposed rather than turned toward a wall. She believed curtains were for the most part unnecessary, preferring blinds in a pinch. At one point when she was selling a house, the potential buyers passed on the property, but wondered if she might be available to decorate whatever house they did find. In her work as a psychoanalyst, she brought order to interiors of an abstract nature.

When my children were little, she engaged with them in a way that authenticated their autonomy. Being too mired in day-to-day tasks, I don't think I understood this dynamic at the time nor did I admire it to the degree it deserved.

In grade school, my son, Nick, loved mud and speed and noise. When called upon to express his opinion in short essays, he declared himself dead set against homework: "It makes me miss most of the Celtics when they're on TV. There's better things to do. It takes too long. It's a waste of time. It's too hard. It's very frustorating [sic]. There's lots of stress, it's boring, it's no fun. My sister messes it up."

"Should Recess Be Longer?" was the title of another composition.

The answer, in short: "Of course it should."

He could cite only one drawback: "Like for example if you didn't have a longer recess you would learn a little more. But personally I don't care."

Another essay stated: "If I am able to get a dirt bike, I would have a path that went around my house. My bike would be a Kawasaki. If I get a dirt bike, I would not tease my sister ever again. I would clean the dishes. I would ride my bike to get donuts. I would empty the trash."

One time, he took his appeal for a BB gun all the way to the kid version of the Supreme Court, to his grandparents.

Lydia wrote back:

I am late in answering your wonderful letter about your urgent wish for a BB gun.

I am sorry to be late. Here are my thoughts and feelings about what you said.

First and most important, I thought your writing and how you expressed your ideas were beautiful. You have good ideas, well stated and well spelled. It is a prize letter. I have said that I would pay you one dollar ($1) a page for a story. Your letter comes so close to being almost a story about your feelings and wishes that I am enclosing double the amount. You wrote four pages. That would be eight dollars. That is too difficult to put into an envelope, so I am enclosing two five-dollar bills. Okay?

Now for how I feel about the things you had to say. What I think may be quite different from what others might feel or think or argue, so you can put it all together in your mind and work it out with your mom and dad.

I am all for dreams coming true. Some, I guess, more than others. But dreams should not be at the expense of such promises to be sooooo good as you did in your letter. You would be an impossible person if you actually were as good as you promised to be. Nobody could always, all one's life, be nice to a brother or a sister. It is terrific to try, and it is helpful to everyone. But occasionally being mean and nasty comes with the job of living and being a human person.

From what I know about you, you'd be very responsible with a BB gun. But the question is not so much if you know how to behave with a BB gun as it is whether or not your parents want the responsibility of your having a BB gun. Guns do cause lots of accidents, yet there are generations of young boys who want to learn to use and have fun with them. It is a very difficult problem for parents. Like many things in life (cars, motorcycles, fishing rods) they're okay if nothing goes wrong and terrible *if something does go wrong.*

When Princess Diana died in a car crash in the summer of 1997, Lydia drafted a letter to the *Boston Globe*, which for some reason was never sent and instead simply pasted in the logs:

Of all the things said and written about Princess Diana's life and death, David Shribman's article "Already, Britain Is a Different Place" is the most powerful, insightful, and beautifully written. In the small world of family and friends, and in the large world around the globe, there seem to be two groups: those who "get it" and those who don't. "It" is the imperative and recognizable need for symbol and metaphor, ritual and pageantry, heroes and heroines, story and fantasy in the lives of the highest and the most humble of individuals. Those writers and non-thinkers are concrete and cannot see beyond their choice of "data" in their thinking and intellectualizing re Diana. There is such a poverty

of imagination and jejune understanding of life. The British mon-
archy, far from being dead, has been infused with new life. In her
life and death, Princess Diana gave it a necessary transfusion.
Thank you, David Shribman.

Lydia was without doubt the most *definite* woman I had ever
encountered.

She had two words she could not stand: "just," when it is
used to belittle something that is important, and "appropriate,"
when it is used as an excuse to do something you don't want to do
but think you should even if you feel it is wrong. Every year on
her birthday she gave up something she did not like or thought
was unnecessary: Lent, in reverse. One time she gave up making
excuses. Before she moved to assisted living and her social life was
curtailed, she gave up always being the one to initiate the conversation at formal dinners, and she gave up dinner parties with more
than ten people in attendance. She said she would no longer attend
what she called "résumé funerals," at which the deceased's public
accomplishments are emphasized at the expense of any sense of his
or her personal relationships.

She did not like wind chimes because she believed nothing
should compete with the sound of nature.

She claimed to never once return a gift—not even the lemonade pitcher I gave her that had a red, white, and blue Stars and
Stripes theme. Never a flag-waver, she thought the colors were too
obvious. Patriotism to her was private. It was the act of sitting by
and waiting with her young family when her husband stood up to
bullies in the South while armed men, on the wrong side, looked
on. It was witnessing the physical deterioration of your elderly

husband, a process accelerated by the deprivations of prison camp, and bending down to tie his shoes when that maneuver was no longer in his power.

She must have had a certain degree of insecurity because she sometimes went out on a limb to be controversial. For instance, one of her bugaboos was Mother Teresa, whom she believed was a fraud who convinced the afflicted that their unmitigated suffering would get them a better berth in the next world while she herself took advantage of every single possible comfort in the Western medicine bag of tricks.

One time her husband was asked by some pro-choice supporters to issue a learned opinion about why abortion should remain legal. It was not difficult for him to come up with a statement thick with caveats and other impressive linguistic artillery. Lydia listened while he read his ornate opinion out loud and then said she wished someone had asked her for her opinion, which was "If men want to tell us what we can or cannot cut from our bodies, it's fine as long as we can tell them what to cut or not cut from theirs."

Oh, she was a strong taste, but I took pride in having her as my mother-in-law. I had heard other women talk about their mothers-in-law and none sounded as appealing, certainly not the woman with only one topic, her macramé, nor the long-divorced woman who liked to exchange unsolicited intimacies with her daughter-in-law ("Isn't it always awkward, the first time you sleep with a man?"), nor the stay-at-home mom whose single joy in life was to deposit enough money in new bank accounts to win a prize, and thus every room of her home was overridden with free toasters, waffle makers, and coffee percolators.

In the summer of 1996, Nick and Lydia celebrated their fiftieth wedding anniversary with a small dinner at the Point with their four children and spouses, six grandchildren, and one nephew, Phelps Stokes Hawkins (PSH), along with his wife, Sandra Lea Earley (SLE), and their son, Robert Bradshaw Stokes Hawkins (RBSH). For the record, many members of the family often referred to themselves by initials. At times I felt as if I had married into the Monogram Lobby.

The weather that weekend would have been worse only if the storm had lived up to its promised status as a hurricane: the water came down in daggers, trees bent sideways, thunder roared. It was a wonder that the road did not wash out. As the outdoors was doubled over in darkness, even at midday, we held a trivia contest in which the members of the family guessed the answers to fifty questions that had to do with family history, courtship, and sibling warfare.

"What did Grandfather do the summer after high school in 1939?"

"He took a bike trip to France with his friend Ward and a boy who died in World War II. They ate tripe."

"Where did he spend his junior year abroad?"

"As a POW at Stalag Luft III. He read two hundred books supplied by the Red Cross."

"What was Grandmother's mother the first to do?"

"As a reporter for the *Knickerbocker News*, she was the first woman allowed into the press gallery in Albany to cover the state legislature."

"What was the name of Grandmother's first crush, the caretaker at her family's house on Pearl Island in the Adirondacks?"

"Tuffy."

"What was the most missed item when the family lived in Switzerland for a year?"

After several false wild guesses and one good one ("the dogs"), the answer came in the form of Anne's pacifier, a small clown called Wawa with a long dunce cap with a nipple on the top. It had been lost in transit by accident, creating a tumultuous time for the youngest member of the family.

Anne: "Still paying for it."

"What dead Austrian does Grandmother think wrote *The Book of Life*?"

"Freud."

"What is the real color of Grandmother's hair?"

Lydia: "White with splotches of gray."

"What dance step was Grandmother famous for when she lived in Washington?"

Lydia: "The Monkey."

"What is the secret to a long and happy marriage?"

John: "We ought to make them answer that secretly in an isolation chamber."

Anne: "It's only forty-eight hours. We can give them the perfect family they wished they had."

Later Lydia wrote this formula for a happy marriage in one of the logs:

(1) *Find a man with a strong chin, a huge head with room for a big brain, and a large heart, who believes that "life is an outside job."*

(2) *Find a woman, almost totally original, who acts out for him all his wild and creative secret wishes, who loves him and*

*produces with him some truly glorious children, who breaks
all the rules/laws he upholds, who believes in vibes and auras
and that "life is an inside job," mix that up, and assure that
each one is responsible for his or her own happiness and then
you top this with joy and you have fifty years plus!*

Lydia was the guiding force behind one of the best parties ever at Thumb Point. She used the excuse of her eightieth birthday party to hire a local company to prepare an indigenous clambake, the kind that the Wampanoag tribe has practiced for hundreds of years. All day, a low-grade fever of anticipation as first the tent was pitched, and then the tables set, and the pit dug. Rocks were placed in the bottom, a wood fire was started, and, when the heat was steady, the food was placed in layers: potatoes first, then corn, then fish and clams and lobster at the top, all of it covered with seaweed so that the entire meal steam-cooked over the course of about five hours. We had eight tables for ten people each in a clearing. Each table had a different color cloth and a centerpiece of brightly painted coffee cans containing wildflowers assembled in such a way that they embodied the casual grace of dancers who radiate perfection even when they slump.

As a finale, Lydia had all the August babies (of whom there were many—the children of late summer who come from love in the early winter) get up and dance to "Zombie Jamboree" sung a capella by the Vineyard Sound. The guys in the group—many of them music majors at their schools, who thrilled at the luck in spending an entire summer being paid to sing on an island at public events, parades, and private parties—had their routine down pat. After several "free encores," they helped themselves to food and drink and put up with older adults telling them either about the fun they had at their age, or the fun they wished they had had.

I think Jane Austen said this, but if she did not, as Miss Pith, she should have:

Everything happens at parties.

I looked around that night and realized that at certain signal moments the people you gather and the place where they assemble can be in and of itself a work of art, as real as any painting in a museum.

The built-in vanishing act underscored the power of the moment.

"The greatest heartache about getting old," Lydia once wrote, "is wanting so much, *yearning*, to be around and to see and be with the next generation, with their talents and passions and possibilities and graduations and passages and achievements and joys and knowing you can't or won't be there."

But since you can't celebrate a major wedding anniversary or a milestone birthday every year, the next best bet for Lydia was the annual feast in which she and her guests got to name their lobsters after people who had offended them in the preceding year. Then the lobsters were thrown into the roiling water. Many families have their own rituals, an annual bonfire or a final hike, some moment of togetherness to mark the season and then to treasure later during the bleak winter months. In *The Big House* by George Howe Colt, the author describes how his family on the Cape had an elaborate ceremony for saying good-bye to departing guests, with everyone gathering on the capacious porch, known as the piazza, waving white hankies and simulating end-of-the-world sobs as a final salute. Once a year, one of our neighbors, David Lewis, supervised his own fireworks display. Each time he detonated colorful crackling sprays of light, he would say, "Now that's popcorn, eh?" The men played with fire, while the women and children sat to the side and watched. Across the pond near the red barn, a family used to have a reunion every first weekend in August, when tents bloomed all over their property. On Saturday afternoon, they would have a wooden boat derby. (Somewhere along the line that stopped, and another annual marker bit the dust.)

Boiling the lobsters was our annual marker.

Before the sacrificial crustaceans were dropped in the huge pot, we named them after players on the world stage.

"Ross Perot."

"Rush Limbaugh."

"Bob Dole."

The honorees on this virtual hit list varied from year to year, though Ken Starr, to his distinction, made it twice.

So once a year, on an appointed summer's evening, our hearts and minds filled with the weight of tradition and the desire for ceremony, we gathered for the execution of a horde of orange animals with claws cuffed by rubber bands, scuttling as best they could to avoid their fates.

Lydia supervised the bestowing of the names.

One year it was Florida representative Katherine Harris.

Another time: "Antonin Scalia."

You could also name a lobster after a sweeping category if you wished.

"Corporate executives who deprive workers of a living."

"The Supreme Court, most of the time."

"Religious fundamentalists."

"All pharmaceutical companies."

Of all the boilees, the most controversial was the Supreme Deity.

When Lydia threatened to drop a lobster named God into the pot, there was a stunned stricken silence among her guests.

(Later my nephew asked, "Is she a Satanist?" "No," John told him, "she's an analyst.")

After God almost got boiled, I did start to worry.

What if she branched out and starting boiling people I had no grudge against?

Say, Mother Teresa, that thin wisp of a woman, of all the people to pick on. It did console me to think that Mother Teresa might not mind her night as a lobster, offering it up as one more indignity on the road to canonization.

Surely, Lydia had limits.

Sometimes my Catholic upbringing would intrude upon our exchanges and I would, to my surprise, hold my ground in fond, fierce, and loyal memory of what that world once meant: the incense and the kneeling, the wafer and the chalice, the priest and the cross, the sermons and the penances, all of it coming toward me in a jumble of images and memories. *No, no, not the pope.*

Lydia told me not to worry.

"I've given up on naming the lobsters."

"Why?"

"It hasn't worked. Most of the people I boil are still here. I think, instead, we should make up colorful curses each time we drop a lobster in the pot."

She is the author of one of the best curses ever, a vintage curse, with pitch-perfect cut-to-the-chase venom.

One time the house was robbed, and as so often happens the worst aspect was not the items that were missing (trinkets really, worth nothing on the open market) so much as the sense of violation.

Lydia filed her version of a crime report in the log:

The weekend we discovered the break-in was so awful. We spent the time venting our frustrations and irritations, getting mad at each other. What stupidity arguing whether Nick was right that they were an off-island couple taking our stuff for resale or I was right they were an island couple decorating their shack for the summer.

They wiped out most of the books, tapes, record player, salad bowls, cooking pots, children's toys. Everywhere we looked something was missing.

Then the curse, which in an outburst of discretion I shall not repeat: suffice it to say it caused our friend Phil to whistle in admiration when he heard it. His eyes lit up, and, grinning, he offered his highest compliment, "That's positively Sicilian."

Chapter Thirteen

"She Is Not So Young Now"

Despite the idyllic veneer, the Vineyard is not without troubles and not without sorrow.

A commentary by Jim Malkin in the *Gazette* made note of the local tendency to "'special' this place to death," quoting West Tisbury selectman John Early.

"Yes," Malkin wrote, "we are lucky to live on this Island. It is special. But sometimes our focus on the special ignores the other side of this Island's coin. Life here is not all farm fresh eggs, salty fishermen, fresh venison and generous camaraderie. There is life here with domestic violence, alcohol and substance abuse, hunger, cold and untreated illnesses."

Every year, every summer, every winter, the worst happens. Tourists crash on their mopeds, an island landscaper succumbs to tularemia (an acute infectious disease also known as rabbit fever), or high school kids, thinking they have an age-related immunity from danger, engage in a drag race in which a high-speed passing maneuver causes their car to flip four times over a distance of 320 feet before stopping (no seat belts). A man, a trusted island worker, caught out in an elaborate Peeping Tom scheme involving a video camera trained on a shower in a rental unit he owned, kills himself rather than face the consequences. A drunk luxury boater runs over his friend in Edgartown Harbor.

The Vineyard shoreline is where the effects of JFK Jr. and his wife and her sister washed ashore after their plane crashed. After several days of false hope, someone said, "Kennedy, whose fate has been to be born into a family with everything and live life with a constant losing of everything, yet to still have everything expected of them." A stranger at Alley's, shaking his head at the headlines: "And I thought my heart could not be broken again." Ted Kennedy eulogized his nephew: "We dared to think, in that other Irish phrase, that this John Kennedy would live to comb gray hair, with his beloved Carolyn by his side. But like his father, he had every gift but length of years."

The greatest source of pleasure is also the greatest source of menace, the water itself. Riptides occur with some frequency, and most people make the mistake of fighting them when the best approach is to go with the flow and, once you have been swept up to hundreds of yards out to sea and the rip expends itself, stay afloat parallel to the shore until you have the energy to swim back.

It seems as if every year someone writes a letter to the editor thanking a stranger for quick action in the face of danger, such as this one addressed to "The Man Who Saved a Life," which appeared in the *Gazette* on August 9, 1994:

Thursday, late afternoon, my daughter nearly lost her life in the strong and unpredictable surf at the ocean beach locally called Painted House off Moshup Trail in Gay Head. If not for a man who heard my daughter's cries and saw her useless struggle against the ocean's current, she would be gone.

He went into the surf to pull her out. She had swallowed water, was panicking, out of breath and way too far out to swim in. She said he was very strong. He was also very lucky and courageous because the sea can take anyone, quickly and without warning.

While she thanked him profusely and assured him she was all right, in her anxiety and fear, she did not ask his name . . . I would like very much to thank you.

You saved many more lives than you know. You saved a young woman, full of life and opportunities, preparing to leave home in three weeks for college. . . . She is not so young now.

One August day began in a spirit of jubilation: we stood on the deck gazing through binoculars at the commotion on the distant lip of beach. The cut was being opened! Trucks had assembled; equipment was readied. To be there at its inception and to have that coincide with the start of our two weeks was a singular stroke of good fortune. For years we had been accustomed to experiencing the cut at the tail end, for a few brief days or so. But now we would have the greedy all of it.

After the usual scramble for sandwiches, drinks, towels, life jackets, water shoes, and sun block, we parceled ourselves out to the various modes of transportation. My favorite was a series of maneuvers that involved swimming a few hundred yards with a towel and hat and sunglasses on my head from one bank of the pond to another; walking across a sandbar filled with muck; passing the house with its pile of rocks in the water covered with netting to preserve its shoreline, past the house that retail genius Mickey Drexler built when he was CEO of the Gap, which resembled (on purpose) an upside-down boat with the rudder on the roof, past the staging area for where the Trustees of Reservations run kayak trips on the pond, clinging to the shore's edge and avoiding the sharp edges of oyster shells and crunchy ignominy of crab carcasses; and finally after twenty minutes or so arriving at the beach on the pond side.

Others took kayaks, canoes, motorboats, Sunfish, or even swam.

When we all got there, we observed that instead of the benign trickle we expected, the water in the cut was similar to that of class five rapids, resembling a bowl of disembodied fists flailing at one another. We told the children, who kept their grumbling to a minimum, that they had to swim on another part of the beach until the water calmed down. It would probably take days.

Not much later, we saw a crowd gather with stricken expressions, hands over their mouths, and others pointing out to sea with looks of mounting horror.

The next half hour passed both in slow motion and with excruciating swiftness. Some stood by, helpless. Others attempted to rocket out by boat to where a man who had fallen in the cut had been tossed to sea. When it was obvious the man did not make it, we all, strangers and friends and family alike, left slowly by common assent, in clumps, moving toward the sailboats or canoes or the path that brought us there, in silence.

Later, a guest named Dan Halgin (now a professor at the University of Kentucky) wrote:

At the time of the tragedy, I was boogie boarding with Jason G. and Nick. I noticed that a mob of people had assembled staring out into the horizon. Thinking that I had a chance to see a whale I quickly made my way to the collection of boys on the shore. I grabbed the binoculars only to see the people weren't staring in amazement. They were staring in fright at the head of a man in the distant sea.

Within minutes a young man (earlier mocked for his haircut and clothing) was able to row out to where the man was last seen. The current's strength was far too strong and within minutes the head was no longer visible.

As the facts were being compiled, I could only think of who the man was. An hour earlier I was talking with an older man that asked me about the cut. The man even joked about jumping in to save a young girl that was walking too close to the water. It was all amusing then. The waves seemed like an amusement park ride, and even though the sheriff had advised people not to go into the water, no one seemed to be in any danger or to view the cut as anything that could hurt someone. Things quickly changed.

Jason, Nick, and I all contributed to the rescue effort. We helped drag boats from the pond to the ocean. We did everything we could but our efforts could not save the man.

The next day going to the beach had an eerie feeling. The tracks from trucks and four-wheelers reminded us of the previous

day's trauma. A life had been taken and the ferocious cut was
back to being like a carnival.

After entering the cut, the man stumbled, then appeared to
regain his footing several yards offshore, only to be overcome by
a strong wave that quickly carried him out to sea. Emergency calls
were made on cell phones, rescue boats launched, and a Jayhawk
helicopter was dispatched from Otis Air National Guard Base on
the Cape. A rescue diver jumped from the helicopter as it hovered
ten feet above the water and then was hoisted back on board in
a sling carrying the man. CPR didn't work. The victim turned
out to be a much-loved high school teacher of mathematics on
the island known for quoting e. e. cummings and Dylan Thomas
and for reciting Dante from memory in Italian, according to the
Gazette, which also reported that he inspired the college admis-
sions essay of a former class valedictorian who went on to Duke.
He ran the scoreboard for the ice hockey games. He drank beer
with the Portuguese fishermen. He was cited as the reason many
of his former students became teachers.

A week or so later at the same beach, we saw some men from
a distance, awkwardly overdressed in shoes and slacks. They were
approaching other bathers, gesturing with their hands.

They wanted to talk to anyone who had been on the beach
the day of the drowning. They wanted to see the cut for themselves.
Before they got there, they could not understand how a man had
drowned when there had been so many people on the beach. It
helped them to see the terrain and gauge for themselves how long
it would take for even strong men to hoist a boat from the pond
side to the ocean, and then power it through the water to where

a person might be in trouble, and how rough the water could be, even on an unrough day.

They were the brothers of Louis Toscano, asking why.

Later Justine wrote about what she recalled from the day in an essay titled "On the Beach," inspired by Thornton Wilder's *Our Town* in which Mrs. Gibbs offers her daughter the chance to relive a day of her choice after she had died: "Choose an unimportant day. Choose the least important day in your life. It will be important enough."

The essay:

Since seeing that play with my family last winter, I often wonder what day I would relive if I were to die tomorrow. Given the opportunity, I would be tempted to choose a day that I remembered clearly, like a wedding or championship soccer game. Suppose I chose a day that seemed to contain no importance to the mind's eye, a day that started as substantial solely because it was just like yesterday, or tomorrow, or even today? But then something happened which gave it meaning.

In my play, the day is a Tuesday—late August, 1995, the beginning of an annual two-week visit to my grandparents' house on Martha's Vineyard. The sky is blue and the sun is hot against my nine-year-old bony and undeveloped shoulders. My hair is knotted and tangled, my face a bright shade of fluorescent red. I am the definition of happiness. I remember waking up at eight o'clock that morning and running down to the shore to put my feet in the warm water. I dug my toes deep into the mud and watched the black sand that lay underneath its lighter brother erupt in clouds of confusion.

It was a summer of youthful fun: potato salad and corn on the cob with cousins, playing tag with new friends, or throwing sand on my brother's friends as they slept on the beach. Later there would be summers of love or summers of adventures, but this summer was one of innocence.

When I was nine, I thought that in my past life I was a seal and that that was the reason why I loved the water. On that particular morning, as I watched the sky and the ocean blend into a similar shade, I noticed that the water was lower than usual. It didn't take me long before I knew why. The cut was finally opened.

When the water level gets too high in the pond by my grandparents' house, a cut is made in the strip of beach that separates the ocean from the pond. This creates a rush of water, moving so fast that it forms what my mother used to call nature's amusement park ride. When I was nine, I lived for this day when pond and ocean united as one.

By the time my family arrived at the beach, it was about noon. Boogie boards and sand castles littered the sand. I remember seeing a teenage boy flexing his muscles at the girls that surrounded him. At the time I made a face and repeated in my head how I never, ever, ever wanted to grow up.

This day I chose, this late August day when I was almost nine and a half years of age, was perhaps more significant than your average day on the beach.

This day at the cut, I saw a man drown, who was but a few years older than my own father, whose hair had only begun to turn the silver shade of gray that marked aging.

This sunny, perfect day, I saw a man lose his life to the water which I thought I knew so well. I would imagine that when most people see a man drown their hearts fill with anxiety and they work in a panicked fashion. But my reaction was different.

I was the only person to move closer and closer to the shore, drawn down to the edge in the moments after his head slipped from view. People shouted, people cried, people dashed to get boats for a rescue, but no one noticed me sitting with my feet stuck in the mud and my hands over my ears. It was a moment of many things: fear, anxiety, stress, but mostly of death.

This is what I remember with my nine-year-old eyes: I saw the man get caught in the current created by the cut. For a second he seemed to lose his balance, and then suddenly he was swept away from the beach by a riptide. His arm came up once as if pleading for help, and then he disappeared. Time on the beach went from benign and joyous to terrifying. In the churning water, could he have lived thirty seconds? A minute? Five minutes?

It wasn't long before the Coast Guard helicopter roared overhead. It was still too late. When they lifted the man's body from the water, I could see his limbs hanging limply, lifelessly.

Most people felt sadness, worry, disbelief, when they saw the man slip from the water's surface and plunge deep into the darkness of the unknown. I, however, felt only betrayal. The ocean had cheated me of my trust. It had shown me that a current has two personalities, the lion and the lamb. That night I went home, listening to countless reconstructions of the story from my parents or my brother and his friends. Telling their own variations, making themselves become the heroes, describing emotions which seemed far from the truth. I spent the night quietly. But in the morning when it became time to go back to the beach and the cut, I was unsure if I ever wanted to go back again. But the day was hot, the sun was strong, and the water glistened in the distance. And before I knew it, I was back on the beach, with my feet buried in the sand.

In *Our Town*, Emily Gibbs relives her twelfth birthday, and when she looks back on it, she realizes that life is filled with moments of importance that go unrecognized. The reason I would go back to the day I saw a man drown when I was only nine years old is because I saw it for what it was. A moment filled with life's lessons—what was ordinary became extraordinary. It was the best day, it was the worst day, and in some ways, it was a day that taught me to see things for myself.

Chapter Fourteen
Time to Leave

Nicholas deBelleville Katzenbach's death in May 2012 was not unexpected.

Six months before, on day two after moving to assisted living, he had arranged for his dog Jazz to join him. In the middle of the night, trying to take Jazz outside, Nick stumbled. He required emergency hip surgery, after which he never regained his mobility.

In honor of his life, Lydia arranged for a "gathering" (*not* to be called a memorial service), held at Richardson Auditorium in Alexander Hall on the Princeton University campus. The front of the program featured a photo of him, hands clasped, looking pensive, a sly light in his eyes. The back cover showed both Nick and Lydia in their prime, wearing lambskin jackets, walking along the canal in Georgetown with their dog King, smiling under a canopy of bare trees, three bicyclists gaining on them in the distance.

William Bowen, the former president of Princeton, thanked Nick for his service as a trustee. When Princeton created a list of its one hundred most distinguished alums, he was ranked at number sixteen. John used to say, "Dad, if you had only tried harder, you might have made it to fifteen."

Herb Sturz, an old friend, told dog stories, about an Irish setter named Mac, Nick's wedding gift to Lydia, who slept under their bed on their wedding night. He mentioned Beo W. Ulf, the St. Bernard, and Willie B., named after Sir William Blackstone, author of the phrase: "It is better that ten guilty persons escape than one innocent suffer."

He said Nick didn't like talking about himself so he didn't, but he listened carefully and drew no distinction between "older people, young people, and dogs. He particularly cared about dogs. Nick particularly liked underdogs. And he had a sympathy for misfits and waifs—and he sure cared about Lydia. It took a great man to win and hold Lydia's heart."

Sturz also said that whenever you asked Nick how he was, he would say, "Just fine." Even during the six months of rehab that went nowhere, he would say, "'Just fine!' And then he wasn't fine."

Jack Rosenthal, Nick's speechwriter from his Washington days, later head of the editorial board of the *New York Times*, recalled Nick's favorite story from a formal D.C. dinner, when the wife of the former president of France, trying to make polite conversation, speaking in heavily accented English, said, "What I wish most for in this world is a penis."

A stunned shuffling of forks, eyes glued to plates, until at last her husband, Charles de Gaulle, broke in to say, "My dear, I think it's pronounced *happiness*."

(A passing truism: in moments of solemnity, if you think the crowd can take it, bring up a body part or function in the hope of bringing the house down; it often works.)

Lydia did not speak, but all four children did.

Christopher remembered asking his father how he survived in POW camp and Nick said he told himself that "the war would surely be over in four months, and he could surely make it four more months. And when those four months passed, he made the same deal with himself for another four months, and again and again."

John imagined his father being welcomed into a secular version of the pearly gates: "I could envision the gates swinging open, only it wouldn't be angels there to greet him. I saw Jefferson and Adams and Thomas Paine; I saw Lincoln and Roosevelt, Justices Frankfurter, Warren, and Marshall, attorneys like Clarence Darrow and Tom Barr. I saw MLK and, of course, Bobby and Jack and Teddy, followed by LBJ . . ."

He saw his father tossed into a heaven where he could "spend his eternity arguing subtleties and nuances of the law that he loves with all the minds he respected, as he patiently and characteristically waits for the rest of us to join him."

Anne remembered her father's advice that she said stemmed from his days at Exeter as a goalie on the hockey team: "Expect the worst—if it happens, you'll be prepared—if it doesn't, by my father's calculation, you will be twice as happy. Along with a beautiful middle name, a strong chin, and a habit of reading mystery novels, my dad handed down this philosophy to me."

And then she acknowledged that her father, a Mets fan, disapproved of her allegiance to the Yankees. "One of his deepest disappointments . . . sorry, Dad."

Mimi went last, as she desired, speaking in a confident melodic voice that filled every corner of the room. Using a live tree on the stage as a prop, she addressed the gathering, asking the healers to keep on healing; the people who worked in government to go on governing, to not give up on democracy; and the educators to educate, all in the spirit of her father.

The person who most commanded the room was a rogue speaker, an old frail man who stood up and seized the podium.

Would this be embarrassing?

A good story followed.

Ward Chamberlin, who had been a senior vice president at PBS, said he had come down to New Jersey all the way from Boston, driven by his nephew, leaving well before dawn, because he couldn't let his old friend go without sharing some words of praise and remembering the time he and Nick and another boy, in the summer of 1939, took a three-week bike trip through Normandy and Brittany. History was breathing down their necks, but they didn't know it. In that moment, they were still young and hale and carefree.

Their trip took them through many small, isolated towns that happened to coincide with the Tour de France. They knew the schedule ahead of the racers and, born strategists, they mapped their route whenever possible to reach the Tour destination ahead of the pros. Thereupon, the villagers bestowed on them victory cheers, the smiles of pretty girls, fresh bread, generous amounts of wine, charcuterie . . . at least until the *real* racers showed up, and Nick and his friends disappeared.

My daughter, Justine, was chosen to read a poem by Lydia that included this stanza:

> *Lies are where*
> *TRUTH lies*

To find its way
Through this
And other lives.
So—here's today's
Truthful lie:
YOU'LL NEVER DIE

I always felt shy around John's dad. Whether he chose to or not, he radiated gravitas. If I couldn't bring up at least the Constitution along with "please pass the butter," I feared I was in danger of superficiality.

He had a lawyer's logic down pat.

Once, when Lydia went on a diet and announced that the last five pounds were the hardest, he said, "Tell yourself you have ten to go."

During the Monica Lewinsky/Bill Clinton controversy, I asked him if he thought Clinton was the target of right-wing conspirators.

"Either that, or he is just not being kept busy enough at the office."

John and his sibs used to call him First National Nicholas, in honor of the way he provided. He had the air of someone both stoic and statuesque who would never fail to deliver on a promise.

The story I like to tell most about my father-in-law is when he visited my son's elementary school.

My children grew up hearing the story about how their grandfather, when he was deputy attorney general of the United States, confronted George Wallace.

When young Nick first heard the story, he said, "That Wallace. He sure was a meanie. I'd like to find his house and go beat him up."

"That," I said, "is not precisely the lesson of Grandfather."

When Nick was in the second grade, in 1990, he asked, "Do you think Grandfather would come to my school for a *special* share?" He and some older pals in the sixth grade cooked up the idea of having Nick's grandfather address both classes in a combined forum.

Special shares were the Cadillacs of shares, and they ideally involved a living creature, at least a goldfish or a baby. The ideal special share was a pro athlete. Short of that, an indulgent grandparent would do.

"Sure," I said. "Just ask."

"When?" Nick the Elder said.

As part of their preparation, the sixth graders at Fort River Elementary School in Amherst were shown snippets of a documentary titled *Kennedy vs. Wallace*.

John's father spoke in his usual soft voice with its low timbre, a voice that soothed and convinced at once:

"Back in the sixties black people were treated differently. They were not allowed to eat at lunch counters; they were made to ride in the back of the bus. They were treated as though they were less than white people. President Kennedy wanted to do something about it. And so he ordered the integration of the University of Alabama. But Governor Wallace tried to block the entrance. I knew he wasn't going to move unless I made him do it. He wanted to be stubborn. Haven't you ever told your parents you weren't going to do something you know perfectly well you should do?"

A boy had a comment: "You look younger in the show."

"It wasn't a show. It really happened."

"A lot younger."

A girl interrupts. "No, you're still okay, the same."

A big grin from the speaker: "Oh, that's my girl."

Another question: "Weren't you scared he might fight back?"

"No, I was much bigger. But it was hot. Something you might not have noticed was that he stood in the shade and he made me stand in the sun. And I was tired. I had been up all night. He really annoyed me."

"What happened to Wallace?"

"He is still alive today. And you know what? He recently said he made a mistake. He was sorry for what he had done. You know there is something on that video you saw that is quite important. After Vivian was allowed into her dorm, we went up there and we told her that even though people were afraid there might be an incident now that she was a student at the university, she should come down and eat in the cafeteria with the other students. So she came down, and took a tray, and stood in line, and went for food, and sat down at a table by herself. And right away—ten seconds after—five white girls came to her table and sat down with her, and right then I knew everything was going to be all right. Young people didn't believe in not treating people right."

"It was all the older people, the stupid older people."

As a lawyer, he possessed a gift for making things complicated, with qualifiers and obscure terminology. But he also possessed an even greater gift: the ability to take what is complicated and to make it simple.

After his appearance, the students sent letters.

"Dear Deputy Eternity General," began one letter from a sixth grader. "I thought it would be another one of those boring lectures, but I was FORTUNATELY wrong. You were interesting and clear. Also, I never met anyone from politics in person (unless you count those cardboard President Reagans you can get your picture taken with in Boston, ha ha)."

One student thought it was great that he knew so much about the 1960s and wondered if he knew about the 1970s as well.

The letters from the children in Nick's grade were less businesslike in tone and they contained crayoned drawings, which may or may not have had any bearing on the subject at hand, including rainbows and pots of gold. They claimed to have "rilly enjoyd" his talk and to have been "tot" a lot (more history clearly than spelling). They couldn't believe that that selfish Wallace "standed in the shade" the way he did. One student asked for his "otograf," and another thanked him for "saving us from all the evil people."

But the most treasured response came from his grandson: "Dear Mr. Person with the same name as me: Thank you."

It is clear to me that everybody has his or her own, seemingly universally beloved version of John's dad. For me it was, above all, seeing him on the Vineyard, relaxed.

"Time to leave," says the note from my father-in-law in the logs, the man whose vision this all was, who had the idea and the means to create this haven and then the heart to share it.

Then a list:

- *Close fireplace flue*
- *Lock all doors and windows*
- *All porch furniture inside*

TO THE NEW OWNERS

- *Pull boats way up on beach*
- *Put canoe under deck*
- *Sails, etc., go to middle bedroom . . .*

Most of the chores are done. I have to get a new tire for the Jeep. The gas in the red tank should be disposed of responsibly. Please ask guys at dump. Don't pour it around Thumb Point please. In a way I hate to leave, but it is that time of year, and you can't fend off the passage of time.

Chapter Fifteen
Great Dark Cattle

Packing is such a hit-or-miss activity, so discordant, especially if you are not a naturally well-organized person. One step forward, three steps back, as you get waylaid by thoughts of the past, by a procession of people that stretches back, in the case of this move, almost a half century. In the end it was just John and me, as it had been in the beginning. We, who had loved the house with an extravagant love, would do it the honor of performing its ablutions. No one else had the heart or the inclination or the time.

As I wiped sweat, cursing the heat, much of my adult life and the life of this house flashed before me: I was drowning on dry land. Images paraded by: the strapless navy-blue polka-dot bathing suit from the early years, the extremely sincere ratatouille I would make whenever John's parents arrived, the pink sweatshirt Justine would wear to the beach, Nick's Styrofoam boogie boards that always looked the worse for wear at the end of our visit, the light blue envelope with Kay's invitation to dinner, the challah bread our friend from Miami made from scratch, the sight of the Lewis children coming up our driveway unattended—*living the kind of childhood people had before they were born*—John assembling with hope and disassembling with resignation his fishing poles, the rusty keys to the house nestled on the rusty hook. I felt cranky, put-upon, and filled with caprice. Not the big-time caprice of a Vengeful Deity, resulting in tsunamis and whirlpools, but a lowercase version as I tossed objects into discard piles all over the living room, dispensing death sentences left and right: *this can go* (an old sleeping bag), *that too* (warped centerboards), *and that* (an ugly mug). Beds were tossed, books discarded, bureaus sent to bureau heaven. Someone, unfamiliar with the property and its location, asked if we were going to have a tag sale. At this remote location? Right.

We asked Donald DeSorcy's son Leo, who took over as caretaker after his father became infirm, if he knew any island guys who might want a free grill and some deck furniture and even some kayaks and a motorboat. How many times had we settled into those all-weather chairs on the deck with a drink or a book? How often had we maneuvered the boats back and forth from the beach, father, son, mother, daughter, friends, cousins, siblings, in-laws? These items were not crazy valuable, and it felt better to place them in good hands rather than to Craigslist them to the highest bidder.

Leo's guys—hardy, consoling, just like the workers on the ferries—showed up in their trucks. They sized up the bureaus, the dining table, a handcrafted linen chest that was a beast to lift despite its beauty: Would the women in their lives approve?

We worried about what to do with Lydia's driftwood chandelier, but Leo said he would take it and put it in his barn in memory of his father, who after all had found it in the first place.

Knowing that this moment had been in the works for years did not make it any easier. I ranged from feeling enraged to resigned.

Why were John and I the ones left holding the bag?

Well, someone had to do the job. Think how much worse it would be if we weren't here, on hand for the last rites.

I had among my belongings a story from the *Gazette* written by Mimi's former husband's brother, Joel Harrison, about the sale of their house overlooking Quitsa Pond. The family had lived in it for fifty-two years in the summer, and like our house by the end, it was the worse for wear: "Most floorboards creaked, the electrical system issued occasional threats, the oil tank was rusted, the kitchen was archaic and most beds were worn and uncomfortable."

Like us they thought about renovations: like us, they kept an ongoing punch list they ignored.

The Harrisons worried that their house might be razed and "replaced by something far larger and more lavish," a disheartening prospect.

Joel found himself mourning not only the house, but what he felt was now missing from the island from when he was young.

What's gone are folks like Capt. Donald Poole, Everett's father, who lived with his wife Dorothy on our shared driveway. This crusty character was straight out of a

Melville book to my teenage eyes. If my memory can be trusted, he wore two brass earrings, had an inscrutable, weather-beaten visage, he walked as if he were perpetually on board a rolling boat, never smiled at me and rarely talked. If he saw me in the rearview mirror he would purposefully slow down so that his primeval truck, whose license plate said "Tired," barely moved. He glared and I cowered. Here was a man whose roots stretched all the way back to the whaling days, a time when the Island was the center of a robust fishing industry, back when the very idea of huge summer homes, sold-out ferries, fancy restaurants and pollution were inconceivable.

Every summer the Harrisons invited the Pooles to their annual cocktail party and every summer they refused, but about thirty years into their acquaintance, Mr. Poole approached "Mistah Harrison," who was out in his yard, shook his hand, and thanked him for being a good neighbor, and then walked back home.

In New England, there is no higher compliment. People in New England are not always friendly, but they are *never* fake friendly.

Recently, I asked Joel what had happened to his family's property.

"I was both enraged and heartbroken that every shrub, tree, and piece of my childhood home was torn down and replaced with a tasteless, visual insult that ruined relations with neighbors."

"I fundamentally don't understand the mindset of anybody needing an enormous house with two kitchens and eight bathrooms that is not in keeping with the history and the geography of its environment. Why aren't they more concerned about their neighbors hating them?

"For me it was a personal loss. An era is over and you feel a certain grief not just for our own selfish reasons but for the passing of time. Many people share that feeling in many places, not just on Martha's Vineyard."

We had great neighbors on the Point. Some who had not been inside our house in years made a pilgrimage to shake our hands and to bid us farewell: the Russells, the Lewises, the Sturgises, Margie Marshall, among others.

Old friends from other parts of the island offered to help, but it was easier to go it alone. They could see from my mood that it was wise to tread lightly and to broach the subject of the move in hushed tones. My touchiness made even the politest inquiry cause for snippiness. I was not proud of myself.

"Did you take *the logs*?" they all asked, summoning courage, whispering.

The logs: yes, of course.

Drawn to their pages over and over, to the innocence with which we thought we could stop time, they put me in mind of one of my mother's favorite quotes: "The years go like great dark cattle, driven by the master herdsman, God."

Over the years, we had a huge cast of characters rotate in and out of that house. In fact, I have never known a family to be as generous with a resource as the Katzenbachs were with the house

234

on the pond: they truly spread the wealth. The childhood friends, of Justine's and of Nick's, represent only a handful of the people, young and old, who showed up.

Claire's mother, Dr. Julie Stanton, who has her own house on the island—the one where Jen stayed when she worked at Stop & Shop—swooped in with medical advice so freely and generously that it was like going on vacation with a physician on call. Other friends who dropped by to swim, to boat, to loaf on the deck, often added their two cents to the logs in addition to family members. I found myself glued to their contents, unable to move forward with the tasks of the day: a boat against a mighty current. Three of the early logs were already packed, so my glum review was restricted to only the more recent years.

John's dad on September 30, 1994:

Closing for the winter—always sad . . . September and October are so beautiful. It seems a shame to say good-bye so early. Yesterday and today, bright, cool, sunny with a few clouds . . . scattered cumulus . . . pond bright blue, quite high. The three swans just flew by in close formation, almost over the house, deafening noise, almost as loud as a jet.

Doing a poor job of closing, but taking comfort in the fact that Vineyard Propane assumed we wouldn't be back and turned off the gas. The food in the fridge suffered somewhat, as did I. Also, the dump is not open and so no place to dump the garbage—small matter. I'll speak to Donald.

I love this place and hate to leave it. Someday I won't. On to 1995.

1995
John's dad:

Came up Tuesday with Willie and Belle, arriving on the new ferry. Key wouldn't unlock gate but I got Donald on the car phone and met him at the up-island Cronig's. Some complaints from the backseat for unnecessary delays. Tea Lane Nursery has done quite a good job. Much poison ivy gone. Ticks, ticks, ticks. Anne and Steve arrived Thursday, Anne and Steve did the heavy work. Steve crawled under the house to get the phone properly connected.

Lydia, on July 28:

N and L off to buy groceries for dinner. Sixteen for dinner: Harrisons, Hawkins, Katzenbachs and Farley and David and Sarah. A stop at Poole's for a summer hello and swordfish and Everett's honed wisdom: "This getting old is no fun. My wife tells me to relax. I tell her it takes me twice as long to do half as much with three times the aggravation! When/how am I going to relax!? I'll quit. That's it. It's just too much."

From Lydia, in September:

Leaving: sob, sob! A great summer. Beautiful weather the whole time. The Rogers house bought by a local Mr. E., who plans to put up a 150-foot-long-by-35-wide house for investment and resale. The CEO of the Gap and Banana

TO THE NEW OWNERS

Republic has bought the old house on the Moores' point and will renovate. According to Tony and Margie—nice people. Lucky people.

1996
Lydia:

Memorial Day weekend celebrated in the best way: opening the house. Everything a JOY, even the fact that Donald DeSorcy hasn't done everything he said he would. Only a small blip as he has come up with the most wonderful idea for a ceiling fixture in the living room. Wait till you see it. Love that man.

Canine caution: We took 66 ticks off Willie last night and stopped counting with Belle who had more. GREAT SUGGES-TION: mix 2/3 cup of Skin So Soft and 1/3 cup water and rub all over dog (not in the eyes). This helps greatly in keeping off ticks as we found in our third day.

Not much other news except Mal Jones on his usual rampage . . . changing road . . . yet what would we do without him? Most interesting person on the pond!

Anne, on June 6:

Electricians came. Electricity didn't.

Anne, on June 7:

Electricity.

Anne, on June 10:

Persistent pug pursuit puts piping plover in peril.

John, on June 17:

Why doesn't everyone come up here in June? Three fish. All stripers. Menemsha. Electricity is great. Telephone remains the same as the past decade (i.e., nonfunctioning). But hey, who wants to talk on the phone anyway?

Me:

The Gap House . . . watching every day as it looms larger. Trying to imagine what it would be like to have a cement mixer fall in a hole in your yard . . . misleading Justine with an affirmative answer every time she asked, "If I ride my bike to the Gap House, will they give me free clothes?"

Reading, reading, reading: this summer I had to read hundreds of nonfiction books for the National Book Award, so I found myself at dawn in the living room in a wonderful silence, reading, reading, reading.

Justine:

This year was great at MV. The fog made it hard to do things, but we seemed to always be having fun. It's hard to believe but even dancing around in the kitchen listening to songs while doing chores was fun. There were many things to laugh about this trip.

TO THE NEW OWNERS

1997

Lydia:

As we get older/old it is distressing not to comfortably, or at all, do the things up here we used to do with such pleasure: sailing, beaching, bicycling, picnics, etc. But the beauty here as we sit looking from the deck often makes up for the ache and acknowledgment of more and more physical limitations.

Anne:

To: LPSK
From: AdeBK
DON'T FEEL ALONE. WE'RE ALL GETTING OLDER.
*   IT'S JUST THAT YOU'VE BEEN DOING IT LONGER THAN THE REST OF US.*

From John to our son, Nick, and his friends Ian Hart and Tim Murpɥy, time-stamped twelve noon:

It was not totally your fault that you were late. Nonetheless, you guys missed curfew by over ninety minutes without calling. Consequently, these rules are set:
(1) Curfew is 12:00 a.m. with possible thirty-minute extension, but only with permission.
(2) You three are grounded until Thursday UNLESS you would like to exchange miles for hours. In other words, run from here past the airport all the way to the Oak Bluffs Road turn and back (distance @ 7½ to 8½ miles) and you will not be grounded. No run. No night activities. And I

mean run. No walking, no hitchhiking, no shirking. Any
misrepresentation will land you in trouble. That's the deal.
No negotiations. Eat the cinnamon buns.

XXX

BIG BAD DAD

John on an unhappy moment:

The four hours in Menemsha Creek that Phil and I spent casting
to perhaps a thousand feeding striped bass without hooking one
of the bastards up, especially after arising before dawn and then
marching a mile through the sand.

In the category of quotable quotes:
Nick, about cousin Avery:

That kid sure is smart. He can even tell you about the vision in
a frog. He must watch the Discovery Channel all the time.

1999
John:

Things aren't the same without Nick and his friends. They
may cause trouble, but the energy they have and their enthu-
siasm for all things Vineyard compensate for the occasional
lapse.

On the other hand, this summer has seen Justine become a
bona fide teenager. Her joy with everything—except for Maddy's

short leash—has been a delight. And her friends Jen and Claire were pistols too. It seems to me that no adventure I could concoct on a page of any novel is nearly as great as the adventure of watching one's children grow.

Justine's summer reading (just before starting high school):

Things Fall Apart, A Yellow Raft in Blue Water, *and* Great Expectations.

Things to avoid:

THE OLD STONE BAKERY. Please do not frequent this establishment. They stiffed Nick's friend Adam out of $250. What jerks! Revenge planned.

Justine:

This summer has definitely been the best. Some of the highlights:
      Going to the beach with the boat and being so pathetic that Claire, Jen, and I had to have some kid swim to us and save us. (Thanks, Bobby . . . err, Luke.)
      Listening to the boys recite every single line from various movies, especially Office Space, The Breakfast Club, *and* Liar Liar.
      Things we missed:
      Bullet. We buried his ashes on the Point so he can chase seagulls forever.

Nick:

Some Vineyard Gazette *headlines you may well have skipped over this summer:*

BEAUTIFUL BROWN DOG FEELS UNDER THE WEATHER: OWNER'S MOOD MIMICS

HAPPY COUPLE BUYS T-SHIRT WITH DOG ON IT

SOCCER PLAYER BUYS ONE-HUNDRED-DOLLAR PAIR OF PANTS

(Sources say, "He has legit internal justification for his impulsive behavior.")

NAKED ACTOR ATTACKS HARMLESS COLLEGE STUDENT

2001

Low moments (from me):

A few gray days at the end, the girls want more freedom than I am willing to grant, and of course we miss our old friend Kay.

John's water report:

The Odd Water Summer. Ocean and pond water were great. Faucet water ranged from barely acceptable to nonexistent and back to the barely passable category.

What I have learned about MV (and especially the Point)—that the ability to meet with various hassles and setbacks with good humor is more important than even the weather. But what truly makes this place special is seeing how we all interact with it, different, yet similar in affection. Blah, blah, blah. Too much sappy stuff. Red Sox rule.

Nick's friend Tim Murphy:

Another relaxing summer on the Vineyard. This year rather than party all night we enjoyed the beauty the Vineyard has to offer. Most nights we sat at the Point with a small fire enjoying the company of others and the beautiful view. Although this Vineyard trip was different from past experiences, it was probably one of the best.

Nick's friend Ben Austin:

I'm so glad I'm finally of the age where I can wine and dine with the Katzenbachs. You easily reached my intellectual level after a couple of glasses of Chardonnay. I'm glad you (and especially Phil Caputo) appreciated my martini-making skills. I finally had a beer with you all and I introduced Nick to raw oysters, which means two taboos have been broken.

H_2O report from me:

John is right. We had the well from hell. Brown ooze everywhere. Only plentiful liquid: tears of frustration. Water god Jeff Serusa to the rescue. Life on upswing.

2002
Claire:

Watch out, Trinity College, here I come.

2003
Nick, clearly back from a year abroad:

Four things I have learned about France that America might consider adopting:

(1) *How to eat (and drink.) Okay, New York is the culinary capital of the world. MV restaurants are not. The new joint in Edgartown? bland, uninventive robbery. Who brings appetizers and mains at the same time?*

(2) *How to work less. Vacation: five weeks. Thirty-five-hour workweek. Work? Why work when you have wine, women, and boule?*

(3) *Though his reasons may be slightly skewed, Chirac was right about our monkey president. Where are those weapons of mass destruction? Still hiding with bin Laden, Saddam, etc.?*

(4) *Obligatory topless bathing. Let's go, America. Let's get with the times.*

This was the summer when Ernie Boch Sr. died. When the boys worked for Wheel Happy, delivering bikes, they used to imagine going to his house and the kind of tip they might receive, namely a Chevrolet or a llama.

From the *Gazette*:

Ernest (Ernie) Boch, a successful car dealer who made his year-round home on the Island, died Sunday morning at his house on the Edgartown harbor.

He was 77 years old and arguably the most famous car dealer in New England, owner of a string of dealerships in Norwood. He appeared in his own television commercials and invited customers to "come on down."

On the Vineyard, Mr. Boch was perhaps better known for the massive and sometimes controversial house he and his wife began building in 1981 on the Edgartown waterfront.

Set on 15 acres, the 15,000 square-foot house took five years to construct and, according to news accounts, contained 62 skylights, 17 heat zones, five miles of copper pipe and a wine cellar big enough for 1,102 bottles.

The pavement outside the mansion was all Italian cobblestone, reportedly the largest private installation in the U.S.

His sprawling front lawn became something of an Island landmark because of the llamas that grazed there. On Sunday, the lawn was also the site for an annual picnic for Camp Jabberwocky, a tradition that started 12 years ago.

Remarkably, the Boch family insisted that the party continue even in the wake of Mr. Boch's death just 45 minutes before campers were set to arrive . . .

The picnic lasted until 4 p.m.

John:

No summer in memory has been as electrifyingly hot as this one. Scorcher after scorcher. I think as the years go by that what I most enjoy about this place is the way it constantly evokes memories of simpler, younger times, and moments of great kid enthusiasm. It is genuinely bittersweet to see Justine all grown up (almost!) and not to see Nick, who is working in the city. The island changes, as do our ways of looking at it. Sounds trite, but it's true.

Me, on highlights thus far:

Justine comes home at last, after nearly a year in France . . . spends most of the first forty-eight hours framing her remarks with "Well, you people in the United States." Thanks to Phil and Leslie, a marvelous white device known as a microwave graces a corner of the kitchen. Thanks to Peter Petre and Ann Banks for their gift of panini maker. As Peter says, "When you have a panini maker, everything looks like a sandwich."

2008
Justine:

As always I had another lovely time on the Vineyard. This trip was extra special as I arrived straight off the boat from Paris, France. I can't imagine a better place or way to have returned to the good ole U.S.A. August 14, 2008. This time next year, I will be a college graduate of about eight months. Holy sh!#!!! Good thing I secured that job at J.P. Morgan!

2009
Me:

Arrived on the island two weeks ago today. Three days of hard work followed. Dennis [my brother-in-law] donated his truck and his saw and cut several dead boats in half, then carted them to the landfill. Dryer was making a dreadful sound: Richard Halgin to the rescue, spending a day scouring the entire island for the best buy. Bottom line: go to Crane Appliance on State Road. Tea Lane Nursery managed to weed-whack the Point into a state of trimmed gorgeousness. Many phone calls to Justine in New Orleans as we vicariously experienced the ups and downs of her moving into her first apartment. She has yet to be placed in a school by TFA; tensions abound. Nick is also on pins and needles with several projects. Parents counsel patience—just what children love to hear.

Obama arrives next week. The island is sinking under the weight of related souvenirs and T-shirts. He will be staying a few beaches over. When we say we are experiencing a holiday fit for a president, we are not exaggerating.

2010

From the *Gazette*, about Obama's visit to the Bunch of Grapes Bookstore on August 23:

"He was a very gracious person," said bookseller Joanne Connolly of Bunch of Grapes, who was in the store on Friday morning when the President arrived with his two daughters to fill out their summer reading lists . . .

Malia and Sasha picked up *The Hunger Games* by Suzanne Collins, *The Land of Elyon* by Patrick Carman, *The Red Pony* by John Steinbeck and *To Kill a Mockingbird* by Harper Lee.

Me, in mid-July, 2011 (or thereabouts):

Socially, a calm time. Margie Marshall stopped me on my morning walk and asked me to drop by for a visit. She has retired so as to be with Tony full-time. She said his Parkinson's has slowed him down physically, but not "above the clavicle." Went to Granary Gallery. Contemplated much mischief. Alison Shaw's even better than ever.

2012

Justine, in June:

Able to sneak up to MV with Mom for a few days before heading back to New Orleans. I'm reminded of just how much I love this place and how much it means to me. Strangely, I got a good deal of work done on this "vacation"—something about no internet makes me that much more productive. It's not the same without having a dog here, but Julie brought over Milo so I was able to dote on him accordingly. Soon we will spread Porsha's ashes here so she can play with her predecessor, Bullet, catching seagulls for eternity. Was sad not to have some of my usual suspect friends up for a visit. No Dr. Claire, now a resident at Tulane in NOLA, no Jen (going to UPenn for the last stint of her PhD in neuroscience), and no Mads (studying to be a nurse practitioner at UMass Medical School). I have such impressive friends who are far more practical than I am! I'm lucky. Most of all I miss Grandfather. I know it has been a few years since he was able to come to MV. I know how happy he was here, wearing his cutoffs, cooking swordfish, and playing cribbage with Grandmother. I think he would be happy to know how much I love this little coin de paradis.

2014
Nick:

Two regrets: We should have had a solar lighthouse and photo printer. There are far too few photos in the book lately. Also, I wrote a haiku. But it is inappropriate for the book. Laters, MV!

Julie Stanton, speaking for the whole Lawlor family (her husband, Ted, and daughters, Claire and Hilary), on August 18:

Sadness prevails as I look around this beautiful living room dismantled and packed into boxes. But there is immense gratitude to have shared even a small part of the experience. And comfort in knowing that the friendships that deepened here will continue forever. To paraphrase Rick and Ilsa, we'll always have Thumb Point. The spirit of this place will live on.

Leslie Ware's final "CONSUMER REPORTS RATES THE BEACH HOUSE":

CR has provided some suggestions as to how to ruin the Point: Tear down the house, replace with a ten-thousand-square-foot "cottage" with turret, widow's walk, and moat. Pave the road and add speed bumps and an electric gate with a guard in a uniform. Install a satellite dish for the big-screen TV that goes over the fireplace. Have a fenced heated pool sunk into the beach.

Pave the beach. Buy jet skis and a cigarette boat. Commence daily delivery of the Wall Street Journal *and the* New Hampshire Union Leader. *Finally, charge all guests: $5 to sightsee, $25 cocktails, $50 dinner.*

Best beach house ever. RIP, Thumb Point.

Chapter Sixteen
At Rest

"You can't fend off the passage of time," as John's father liked to say.

As we headed down our driveway to the dirt road, leaving the house behind for the final time, I wondered as I always did when I left for the summer about the island at rest. Was it like the Night Kitchen, all chaos and merriment? Even better? I had visited a few times during the shoulder seasons (late spring just before summer and early fall just after) and once at Thanksgiving, and I got the impression that for year-round residents the real life of the island occurs most vividly any time but July and August.

I once had a student in my memoir class at the University of Massachusetts who grew up on the island. In response to a prompt about "The Things They Carried," Rob Morgan wrote about a piece of wampum from the beach on Martha's Vineyard, explaining that it is "just part of a sea-worn hard-shell clam or quahog. It ranges from white to lavender to a kind of organ-dark purple, which is my favorite. It connects me to the Vineyard and its history when I'm away from it. The first one I carried was given to me by a girlfriend of nine years. She wanted to get married, I couldn't quite commit, and it ended. But I carried that damn shell around for another five years then lost it. I've got a new one now."

If I remember correctly, Rob's father had been harbormaster on the night of Chappaquiddick. You can see Rob in *Jaws*—an extra, along with his sister: little kids bobbing on a raft just before one of the attacks. Because getting on- and off-island always requires forethought, the Vineyard has the capacity to make you feel closed in and trapped. Rob experienced that sense of enclosure to an extreme degree. He said that he was nine years old before he took the ferry for his first trip to the mainland and how he had to catch the next ride back because his mother, who was agoraphobic, had jumped off just before the boat left the dock. Later, smitten with wanderlust, he tried to join the marines and received a letter back from a recruiter, who lauded Rob's high goals and tenacity but said that as an eleven-year-old he did not meet the age requirements. He ended up writing, and publishing in *Boston Magazine*, an essay called "Island Bound" describing how when he finally came of age, he lit out for the territory:

> In 1983, when I was 18, I left the island for the first time. I experienced enormous joy in seeing a world I had known only through stories and pictures. Among other things, I "discovered" at 70 miles per hour what a rotary is. I wondered at the beauty and synchronicity of a traffic light. I marveled at the Boston skyline. I rode an escalator for the first time but didn't know how to work an elevator and was too embarrassed to ask, so I usually used the stairs. I went to 43 states and hitchhiked through California. I

traveled from Mexico to Canada to Ireland to Poland. I lived in Vermont, Boston, and New York, where I worked in film production—a lifelong dream.

Yet Rob reported that it is always a thrill to see Martha's Vineyard from out at sea when coming home on the ferry:

I now live far from the ocean. In the summer I will visit my parents. Leaning against the rail of the boat, I will see the island as a thin line on the horizon. And I know that from where my mother waits, the ferry will look like a dot on the sea. I'll ask my father to take the beach road home. I'll look to my left and find the Atlantic curling into the shore. It has always been my favorite view.

Rob, as a child, and his family to this day, as well as the schoolteachers and the fishermen and fisherwomen and the seafood store operators and the nurses and the doctors at the hospital and the home health care workers and the construction workers and the retired summer residents and the librarians and the school-children, know the true story of the island at rest. My sense is that the Vineyard in winter is similar to the town where I grew up in the western part of Massachusetts: it exults in the rhythms of its ordinariness. People harvest grapes for jelly and they freeze their homemade raccoon stew. Life in the off-season boils down to an elixir of essentials: light and the lack of light; cold, more cold, and what to do about it.

I read the *Gazette* thoroughly, which I suppose is already, from the many references to it in this account, obvious. What a treasure that paper is, both well written and well edited. It is fiercely local. "Names sell newspapers" is an old journalism saw, upheld with enthusiasm by the writers of the six town columns who report on world events rarely, nature and her sermons often, and news of family and friends and neighbors all the time. The paper honors the past, seeing it as an undercurrent that buoys the present. And it is visionary: the paper keeps the island's future front and center with an implicit sense that it is an expendable resource if we don't watch out.

The paper lets me know that by Labor Day the island has cleared out and a more restful rhythm takes over. The invitations from prep schools and posh colleges for cocktail parties are no longer featured in the paper, replaced by ads for winter rentals. Now you can detect sweet pepperbush that attracts bees and butterflies. Sailors love it because, inhaled from out at sea, the odor carries the promise of land.

The first order of business is getting the island children back to school, but also right up there is the annual Martha's Vineyard Striped Bass and Bluefish Derby, which lasts five weeks and features big money prizes in an array of categories, as well as grand prizes like a new Chevrolet Silverado 4x4 and a nineteen-foot Boston Whaler. The men and, increasingly, women (Phil, take note!) talk about past triumphs, a 10.13-pound bonito caught off Nomans Land and the 12.48-pound false albacore caught off Memorial Wharf in Edgartown.

Seasonal residents close up their houses, laying a fire as a final gesture to ensure a guaranteed greeting in the upcoming spring.

The Polar Bears, self-named and perhaps not as intrepid as the winter Polar Bears you read about elsewhere, swim at Inkwell

Beach in Oak Bluffs every morning from the Fourth of July until Labor Day. They bid each other good-bye, remembering among other fine moments the impromptu concert of jazz on a keyboard and flute that greeted them one summer's day.

At Heather Gardens in West Tisbury, if you buy three mums you get one free. Sheep are put out to pasture in fields that were off-limits during the summer months. Monarch butterflies swarm the island in the early fall, competing with the foliage for the prize of most colorful. A powwow might be scheduled in Aquinnah. Stores go out of business or have insane sales.

By early October the recreational season for bay scallops opens. In recent times, two dueling worries: the fear of a sparse harvest and, even then, not enough shell fishermen to get what there is. The diminished supply sickens those who care about such matters. The culprit, they say, is in the Midwest: higher smokestacks carrying more pollution across the belly of America to the coast.

The Chilmark General Store closes until the spring. Some of the fish markets stay open until Columbus Day. The second Tuesday in October is called Cranberry Day, a time when children get a day off from school and families all over the island celebrate not just the cranberry harvest, but abundance in general, with picnics and storytelling and gatherings.

By mid-October applications are available for the Red Stocking Fund, a charity that has been in existence since the 1930s, which supplies food, toys, and clothing to island children through the eighth grade over the holidays.

The commercial scallop season begins sometime in November.

At West Tisbury School, the children traditionally prepare one hundred pumpkin and apple pies for the food pantry and the elderly.

Late fall: shotgun season for deer. Wear bright colors.

The Old Whaling Church holds an annual holiday concert.

A Festival of Wreaths benefits the 1832 Sara Mayhew Parsonage in Edgartown.

All winter, new babies are welcomed: Stella, Tabitha, Eagan.

In the spring: witch hazels, camellias, magnolias, rhododendrons, viburnums, dogwoods, and, just before summer, just before the population swells from 15,000 to 120,000, stewartias.

Around May first, Morning Glory Farm reopens, advertising "young and lusty plants."

The orioles usually return just in time for Mother's Day.

The students at the Chilmark School distribute May baskets to members of the community, with the fourth and fifth graders performing the maypole dance. The Chilmark Community Church celebrates the annual Blessing of the Fleet on the Sunday of Memorial Day weekend. According to the town news one year in the *Gazette*:

> The service begins at 9 a.m. in the parking lot next to the Menemsha Texaco building. All are welcome at no cost and the children are made part of the event, to their delight. It is a most enjoyable annual event with music and refreshment and a reading of the list of Menemsha boats.

And every year, if you are a seasonal visitor, you see the changes you might not notice with the same jolt if you live on the island year-round and witness the flux in slow motion: A fishing shack is gone. A mansion has sprouted up on State Road on the corner leading to the beach at Abel's Hill South. The intersection at Barnes Road and the Edgartown–Vineyard Haven Road has a roundabout; it cost $1.4 million and some neighborly goodwill between those who oppose any changes to the island that smack of city and those who don't. (In 2016 the town of Oak Bluffs declared the former blinking light to be surplus so it could be auctioned off at the Possible Dreams auction as a nostalgic icon. A couple bought it for $8,600.)

More and more the houses are architected, like the Gap House across from us, the one with the roof that resembles a rudder. You will know its current owner is on his way when you see landscapers combing the seaweed off the beach in front of the property. Fancy, fancy, fancy.

Also, all over you will see new swimming pools or the equipment to create them: pretty soon the island will be a doughnut.

As to the ultimate question: How much did the new owners pay for our place?

Three million dollars minus $17,000 for our share of their new roof.

You might think that with our portion of the loot from the house, we took off for the Riviera to live in perpetuity on the spoils. Not so fast.

The days following the sale were an exercise in accounting.

Expenses associated with the move came to $13,020.11.

John warned his sibs there would be another bill from Leo DeSorcy.

Our accountant, June Walker, sent a bill covering her preliminary handling of tax aspects of the sale: $3,620. June agreed to prepare a K-1 form for everyone.

"The K-1 forms should go to whoever does your 2014 taxes," John said in a note to his siblings. "Please be prepared to pay the government approximately 20 percent of what you receive from the sale. That's the low-end estimate."

We had been covering expenses on the house through an equity loan for at least five years, so after paying that off, after paying the real estate agent and the lawyers and the accountant, after paying back individual debts to the kitty by those who had borrowed from the estate, after setting aside a wad of cash for the government, everyone had enough to feel better about their bank accounts, but not enough to change any lifestyles. For the most part the windfall relieved debt and created a cushion against the encroachment of our advancing years. This was an amazing gift on top of the memories and nothing to scoff at.

Some of our old neighbors nursed a fantasy that the new owners might allow the land to revert to its wild state and make it a kind of visual public park for everyone to enjoy as they swam or boated by the property.

Wishful thinking.

Most expressed a strong opinion against expansion, hoping to find an old rule somewhere that would prevent any new construction. Someone promulgated a Hail Mary theory: perhaps the riparian owners (the association of people who own land on the pond) had agreed internally fifty years ago to limit the size of new construction to three thousand square feet.

More wishful thinking.

In that first winter season after our departure, snow was record-breaking all across Massachusetts, and the Vineyard was not spared. On the island, most of the barn owls starved to death, as they were unable to feed on the rodents beneath the snow. As a result, Susan Straight commented on the *Gazette*'s website, "the population of white-footed mice (an important vector in the spread of Lyme disease) is likely to sky-rocket."

On March 9, 2015, the West Tisbury Planning Board reviewed the plans for a new house to replace our old one:

> The proposal is to replace an approximately 2000 sf seasonal house with 1969 sf deck with a year-round house of 5054 sf plus 3431 sf of deck. There will be a 560 sf auxiliary structure (garage) located approximately 200-plus feet to the north from the main house.
>
> The original Katzenbach camp was built about 50 years ago and renovated into several structures (detached master bedroom/bath and main house including 4 bedrooms, living/dining room and kitchen plus bathrooms) by DeSorcy Company about 20 years ago. About that time electricity and phone service were provided to the site and to other locations on the easterly side of Thumb Cove—before there was no electricity or phone service on that side of the Pond. The renovations were completed to a very high standard and the rustic style is very charming. Over the years the residence has weathered and the vegetation grown so that the complex is barely visible from the Pond.
>
> The current plan places the location of the current residence (grandfathered) to be located in the shore district of the coastal zone, and the proposal is to locate the new house—which will be a year-round rather than seasonal

house—so that all but a small portion is out of the shore district although the deck is actually significantly greater in size, and thus significantly greater in impact on the coastal zone.

After a description of the proposal by Reid Silva, James Moffatt of Hutker Architects showed the plans and described various aspects of the plan including the general layout, energy efficiency, architectural style, need for special permits, and elevations which show a central flat roof portion surrounded by several components which will have gable roofs. The plan contains 5 bedrooms, 6 bathrooms, a wing with a kitchen/dining room/living room and a central portion containing four closable areas for unknown use. There is also a considerable amount of glass-enclosed space which is peripheral to the main central units.

The applicants' agents were reminded of the demolition delay clause of the ZBL.

Questions were posed by board members, and members of the audience and abutters (Mal Jones and Joel Kirschbaum), about the adequacy of the dirt road leading to the property, about the point's propensity for significant erosion, etc. Virginia Jones commented that the access dirt road can be easily flooded either when the Pond is very high, or during coastal storms. In fact on the point to the west the hurricane line from the '54 hurricane is still visible and on Thumb Point it would be either at, or close to, the base of the proposed house with the access road being flooded.

James Moffatt pointed out that the current plan is for the central flat roof to be accessed by an outside stairway, and roofed by a roof system composed of a waterproof membrane topped by—perhaps—succulents. After considering the design—essentially a glass box with various internally segregated rooms, the applicants were also reminded by the board of the need to minimize light pollution with shaded down-pointing or inward-pointing light fixtures, particularly as the plan shows floor-to-ceiling full glass windows and numerous potentially lighted areas both inside and outside. All landscaping is to be planned with reference to the guidelines established by the Polly Hill Arboretum, no fertilizers or chemical amendments (pesticides, fungicides, herbicides) are to be used, all glass is to be nonreflective and no cutting is allowed in the overlay districts. Heights of the various facets of the structure are strictly regulated and must be designed and constructed according to the heights allowed in the various overlay districts. As shown the plan is currently for red and/or white cedar shingled walls. Roof of gabled areas was not described. Glass windows are planned to be triple glazed although this may be an issue due to inability to meet hurricane standards. Shutters may be required.

As a new septic system and location are required, we urge that a state-of-the-art denitrification system be installed. This is particularly urgent due to the potential year-round use of up to 6 bathrooms by a potential of 10 or more people.

It was suggested that the proposed 12' x 42' pool should be constructed so that when the Pond is flooded that the pool doesn't pop up and float away. Any associated machinery (pool equipment, auxiliary generators, and other noisy machinery) is to be located underground if possible and in highly sound-insulated structures.

Although it was not mentioned, we remind—by this letter—the applicants that any paths in the various overlay districts, or future docks, will need to be reviewed and permits obtained. Any riprapping or coastal armoring must be reviewed and permitted in advance. Further any additional structures for sports equipment, boats, guests, etc., must be reviewed and permitted as well.

The project is being reviewed by the ZBA (height of railings on flat roof portion), BOH, ConCom. We urge each entity to do a site visit and to review this project very carefully in the context of its very fragile location. We believe that there is ample room on the property to locate the structure completely out of the various overlay districts and we urge that the driveway also be located to minimize danger of storm surge flooding.

Our old house—exasperating, endearing, cranky, creaky, dusty, demanding, *ours*—would be no more.

Our friend Leslie was right when she wrote: "Best beach house ever. RIP, Thumb Point."

Fortunately, whenever I lost perspective, I had the perfect move on my chessboard. I would reread what Anne had written in the log on September 9, 2012, a few months after her father died.

John's father always said there might be many places on the earth as beautiful as the Point, but none more beautiful.

I would say there might be people who loved the Point as much as Anne, but none more so.

This island has been a part of me since before I was born. I often picture my beautiful mother so fully pregnant with her last child that summer of 1959. How could she, how could my sister and my brothers, how could my father, imagine what a gift they were going to give me for the next fifty-plus! years. My connection with Martha's Vineyard is my point of balance—here the scale of life, worries, love, happiness doesn't move. The water, the wind, the sand, the sky erase all turmoil, all worry, and bring a happiness to the deepest part of my being. Every sunset—thunderstorm— every beach rose blooming in June, the filling and emptying of the pond when the cut is open and when it closes—these are the things that are more significant markers in my life than birthdays or anniversaries. They underscore the inevitable changes that life brings. Happiness, sadness, changes that we never forget and those that elude us, insignificant in our day-to-day lives that somehow become important on the day we realize we will no longer record them in a log like this.

I am crying. Thank you, Mom and Dad. Thank you for showing me how to love a place, how place stands in for those you love and how it makes you who you are. Thank you, thank you, thank you, thank you for the sand in my shoes, for teaching me to swim and sail and paddle a canoe. Thank you for lobster dinners, swimming naked in the ocean, for letting me sit at the grown-up table, and letting me grow to be an adult here on Thumb Point. Love to Dad: I miss you so. Love to Mom: You and your stubbornness made Thumb Point happen. Love to my brother John. To all the folks that have passed this way. I thank you.

To all the dogs that have had the time of their K-9 lives here, I thank you for showing us clueless humans what joy really is.

Today I stood on the deck at five p.m. in the bright sunshine with rain pouring down and saw a rainbow stretch from beyond the outdoor shower to the other side of Thumb Cove. It was perfect in its arc, vibrant in its colors, and enormous in its reach. All I could think was: Thank you, thank you, thank you.

I counted.

Anne used the word "happiness" not once, not twice, but three times.

Madame de Gaulle would be so pleased.

John had the honor and the obligation of writing the absolute final entry on the last page of the log, as if all the years on the Point had led to this one blank page, waiting to end the ambiguity inherent in its blankness with a message for one and all. It was so perfect that there would be but one page left. It reminded me of the time John's dad took his car in for a thirty-thousand-mile checkup at exactly thirty thousand miles, and the young attendant told him, sweetly, hesitantly, that it didn't have to be *on the dot* to qualify for an oil change, as if Nick were so superannuated he had nothing better to do than drive his car around with the express aim of hitting the perfect mileage for a tune-up.

John wrote:

> *In my writing life, I have written many endings, some of them quite notable, some forgettable. But when it comes to writing an end to our time on the Point, I am at a loss for words.*
>
> *So I won't try to write what this place meant to me, to my family, to Maddy, Nick, and beautiful Jussie, or to our friends who have visited here.*
>
> *And in truth, the memories of this spot really defy any ending coda. So—no final this or that. Good luck to the new owners. I can only hope they have a taste of the joy this spot has provided all for us for so many years. Me—well, Montana? The Adirondacks? Key West? The Glacier Mountains? I'll figure something out.*

Montana, the Adirondacks, Key West, the Glacier Mountains: all terrific places, but none is Martha's Vineyard.

Recently, I thought back to two of the books I gave to Mrs. Graham when she was writing her memoir: *This Boy's Life* by Tobias Wolff and *A Moveable Feast* by Ernest Hemingway. The first book is a perfectly observed story of a child who, despite his mother's best efforts, cannot find a place where he feels safe or welcome, with prose that ranges from the flippant to the lyrical, as in "My first stepfather used to say that what I didn't know would fill a book. Well, here it is." And "This is a book of memory, and memory has its own story to tell. But I have done my best to make it tell a truthful story." The second book, by an old man looking back, recognizes that place can be portable if it manages to seal itself in one's memory with an adhesive force that no tool ever invented (maybe not even senility) can dislodge: "There is never any ending to Paris and the memory of each person who has lived in it differs from that of any other." You don't need to be Lydia the analyst to figure out why those books mean so much to me.

The first summer after the sale, I was already making plans to return. We were invited to visit two sets of friends in July, and that September we attended our first wedding at the Allen farm when Molly Grand-Jean married Greg Heller, who, though both are from New York, met as teenagers working at Larsen's Fish Market, adding a solid island note to their nuptial pedigree. The following summer, in 2016, we returned as renters for a week in June, for Claire Lawlor and Alex Riley's wedding in the same primo venue. (Claire, to whom family friend Phil said upon learning that she was studying medicine, "But you look so young. Who would go to you?" is now an otolaryngologist.) Her engagement to Alex occurred at the lighthouse in Aquinnah: another solid note. They asked John to be their minister for a day. In helping John prep for his talk, the young couple requested that he not discuss medical school, sex, siblings, money, religion, future progeny—topics he then threatened to embrace with brio.

Rain kept us from the sweeping green expanse by the water, where white-cushioned chairs had been assembled in the event of decent if not perfect weather. Relegated to the cocktail tent for the ceremony, the guests maintained a spirit of typical New England fortitude: "At least it's not a nor'easter; at least it's not a hurricane."

John began with a joke about how pleased he was to be the o-fish-iant. As so often happens, the best moment of the ceremony was unscripted. When the time came to place the ring on the groom's finger, it was nowhere to be found. Shrugged shoulders, panicked expressions, and whispered directives followed. Finally, the mother of the bride realized it was in her pocketbook, in the main tent, a hundred yards away. From afar, using hand signals, she mouthed the word "purse" and gestured with a downward fist hoisting an invisible object to the wedding planner, who then took off on a dead run to get it. During the prolonged silence that followed, Claire announced, "This is a hiccup," to which John replied, "I prefer to think of it as a mystical moment," both of which got a big laugh. Then, in a wondrous turn, the bridesmaids eyed each other. And yes, the catchiest of all bridal songs, the one that the young women had been singing during the hairdo and makeup session earlier in the day, took hold, as if by spontaneous combustion: "Chapel of Love." Many in the tent chimed in, and when the out-of-breath wedding planner sprinted back with the groom's ring, the stage had been truly set for getting married.

Vows were spoken.

The couple kissed.

We were all figuring on happily ever after from this point.

As I listened to the beat of the storm, I trained my eyes on the bride, the groom, and the ocean in the gray sodden distance and thought about how lucky I was to be in this setting and to witness all this beauty mingled with goodwill and hope.

The day after Claire and Alex's wedding, Nick flew out, passing over our old property. Nick said it looked like a ton of construction was under way.

A week or two later, I e-mailed an old neighbor: "I can take it: Am I right that our old house is being torn down? I am wondering because when we last spoke, the new owners had gone before the board with their proposal but I had no idea how it turned out."

The reply:

"Ah, I hate to tell you but yes, your wonderful camp is no more. And in its place, a 5,000 sf one-floor (meaning very long) high-end home shoehorned into the wetland boundaries with 5 bathrooms and . . . are you ready . . . a lap pool."

Okay, ouch, but not a surprise. In any event, the property is now theirs to have and to hold.

As for me, the grip of the island on my psyche has not diminished with time and I do not expect it will. The house is no longer ours, yes, but the island will *never* end. And besides, a loss of property is not a loss of life. We should be grateful for all the times we lose land and things and ballast and stuff and merchandise for being stand-ins, for keeping us from the sadness of more profound loss. Anyway, just think: every year, a new summer, coined for us by the earth on its axis, composed of sunshine and indolence, beckons.

I know where I will be, one way or the other.

Acknowledgments

As anyone who has read the foregoing has likely observed, I am possessed of an archival mentality and I have cited many texts besides my own in the creation of this work. I would like to thank all who gave permission to share their words, especially Ron Rappaport, Joel Harrison, Jen Tyson, and the estate of Art Buchwald. Hilary Wall, librarian at the *Vineyard Gazette*, was especially helpful.

Having trained in the world of newspapers, back when they roamed the earth, I am well aware there is no such thing as somewhat accurate. I have done my best to be totally accurate and totally factual. Any mistakes are mine and mine alone.

I have many people to thank for encouraging me in this endeavor. My husband, John, of course, who is a thriller writer. I probably should have mentioned earlier that he set one of his scariest scenes on the Point in a novel called *The Traveler*. My daughter, Justine, proved an astute and exacting early reader, and my son, Nick, gave me his blessing, though he did say that if he were to write a book it would be called "Not for Sale" and it would consist of two words, "The End."

I want to give particular praise to my sister Jacqueline. How many writers are lucky enough to have a sister who worked for twenty-eight years as an editor and writer at Gannett and even in retirement has an apparently undiminished desire to hunt down a missing ellipsis or a misplaced comma? As she is two years and six weeks my junior, this affords her the double pleasure of being both right and superior.

Thanks also to my agent, Andrew Blauner, who is so good at what he does that all my friends have agent jealousy, even the ones who are not writers. He was the force behind my reunion with Morgan Entrekin at Grove Press, who in turn handed me over to editor Jamison Stoltz. Jamison's attentive readings went way above the call of duty. He is tough, but he knows what he is doing.

Finally, I want to thank Nick and Lydia Katzenbach, and their children Chris and Mimi and Anne, and, of course, all their dogs, past, present, and future. They are a remarkable family, and I am proud to be part of them.